SAS® MACRO PROGRAMMING MADE EASY

MICHELE M. BURLEW

Comments or Questions?

The author assumes complete responsibility for the technical accuracy of the content of this book. If you have any questions about the material in this book, please write to the authors at this address:

> SAS Institute Inc.
> Books by Users
> Attn: *SAS® Macro Programming Made Easy*
> SAS Campus Drive
> Cary, NC 27513

If you prefer, you can send e-mail to sasbbu@sas.com with "comments on *SAS® Macro Programming Made Easy*" as the subject line, or you can fax the Books by Users program at (919) 677-4444.

The correct bibliographic citation for this manual is as follows: Burlew, Michele M., *SAS® Macro Programming Made Easy,* Cary, NC: SAS Institute Inc., 2001. 280 pp.

SAS® Macro Programming Made Easy

To Betsy and Penny

Acknowledgments

So many people helped me write this book.

A BIG thank-you to my editor Julie Platt who guided me along this new and exciting road. Thanks also to David Baggett and Jennifer Ginn who for *years* asked me if I was *ever* going to write a book. Thanks to Nancy Mitchell for helping me unravel the design aspects of writing a book. Thanks also to those in Publications who helped produce this book: Sue Kocher, Karen Haley, and Cate Parrish. The feedback I received from the reviewers was invaluable: Nancy Agnew, Carol Gretz, Sue Hakomaki, Susan O'Connor, Heather Russell, Kevin Russell, and Russ Tyndall.

I also want to acknowledge my friends from St. Paul Computer Center at the University of Minnesota, especially Jim Colten, Mel Sauve, Dave Schempp, Karen Schempp, and Terri Schultz. Not only was it fun working with you, but the programming skills I learned—including SAS macro programming—have helped me over and over again.

For their encouraging words, I thank Martha McGough, Janice Jannett (also from St. Paul Computer Center), Jean Burris, and Barb Thill.

Most of all, I thank my husband, John Bauhs, for his support, patience, and "editorial comments" throughout this adventure.

Table of Contents

x

CHAPTER 1

Introduction

Imagine you have an assistant to help you write your SAS programs. Your assistant willingly and unfailingly follows your instructions allowing you to move on to other tasks. Repetitive programming assignments like multiple PROC TABULATE tables where the only difference between one table and the next is the classification variable are delegated to your assistant. Jobs that require you to run a few steps, review the output, and then run additional steps based on the output are not difficult; they are, however, time-consuming. With instructions on selection of subsequent steps, your assistant easily handles the work. Even having your assistant do simple tasks like editing information in TITLE statements makes your job easier.

Actually, you already have a SAS programming assistant: the SAS macro facility. The SAS macro facility can do all the tasks above and more. To have the macro facility work for you, you first need to know how to communicate with the macro facility. That's the purpose of this book: to show you how to communicate with the SAS macro facility so that your SAS programming can become more effective and efficient.

An infinite variety of applications of the SAS macro facility exist. An understanding of the SAS macro facility gives you confidence to appropriately use it to help you build your SAS programs. The more you use the macro facility, the more adept you become at using it. As your skills increase, you discover more situations where the macro facility can be applied. The macro programming skills you learn from this book can be applied throughout the SAS System.

You do not have to use any of the macro facility features to write good SAS programs, but if you do you might find it easier to complete your SAS programming assignments. The SAS programming language can get you from one floor to the next, one step after another. Using the macro facility wisely is like taking an elevator to get to a higher floor: you follow the same path, but you'll likely arrive at your destination sooner.

What Is the SAS Macro Facility?

Fundamentally, the SAS macro facility is a tool for text substitution. You associate a macro reference with text. When the macro processor encounters that reference, it replaces the reference with the associated text. This text can be as simple as text strings or as complex as SAS language statements. The macro processor becomes your SAS programming assistant in helping you construct your SAS programs.

The SAS macro facility is a component of base SAS. The base SAS product is integral to the SAS System and must be installed at your computing location if you want to write SAS programs or run SAS procedures in any of the SAS products. Therefore, if you have access to the SAS System, you have access to the macro facility and you can include macro facility features in your programs. Indeed, many of the SAS products that you license contain programs that use the macro facility.

The SAS macro facility works side-by-side with base SAS to build and execute your programs (Figure 1.1). The macro facility has its own language distinct from the SAS language, but the language and conventions of the macro facility are similar to the style and syntax of the SAS language. If you already write DATA steps, you have a head start on understanding the language and conventions of the macro facility.

Figure 1.1   How the SAS Macro Facility fits into the SAS System

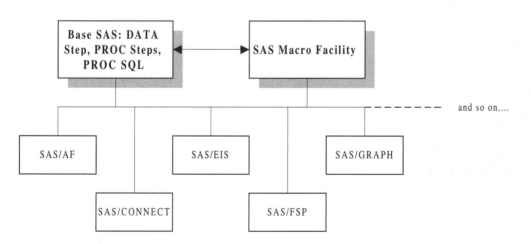

The two main tools of the SAS macro facility are SAS macro variables and SAS macro programs. With SAS macro variables, you create references to larger pieces of text. A macro variable is typically used to repeatedly insert a piece of text throughout a SAS program. SAS macro programs use macro variables and macro programming statements to build SAS programs. Macro programs can direct conditional execution of DATA steps and PROC steps. Macro programs can do repetitive tasks like creating or analyzing a series of data sets.

The following program uses a macro variable to select a subset of a data set. Information about the subset is included in the title. Macro language and references are highlighted.

```
%let mosold=4;
proc print data=books.ytdsales(
                    where=(month(datesold)=&mosold));
   title "Books Sold for Month &mosold";
   var title salepric;
   sum salepric;
run;
```

Next is a macro program that when executed runs a PROC step on three different data sets. The macro language and references that generate the three steps are highlighted.

```
%macro sales;
  %do year=1997 %to 1999;
    proc means data=books.sold&year;
      title "Sales Information for &year";
      class section;
      var listpric salepric;
    run;
  %end;
%mend sales;
```

The macro facility was first released in SAS version 82.3 in 1982. There are few statements in the macro language, but these are very powerful. Compared to other software features, the macro language has changed little since its introduction and relatively little has been added to the language.

In a world of rapidly changing software tools and techniques, the macro facility remains one of the most widely used components of the SAS System. What you learn now about the macro facility will serve you for many years of SAS programming.

What Are the Advantages of the SAS Macro Facility?

Your SAS programming productivity can improve when you know how and when to use the SAS macro facility. The programs you write can become reusable, shorter, and easier to follow.

In addition, by incorporating macro facility features in your programs you can:

- Accomplish repetitive tasks quickly and efficiently. A macro program can be reused many times. Parameters passed to the macro program customize the results without having to change the code within the macro program.

- Provide a more modular structure to your programs. SAS language that is repetitive can be generated by macro language statements in a macro program and that macro program can be referenced in your SAS program. The reference to the macro program is similar to calling a subroutine. The main program becomes easier to read - especially if you give the macro program a meaningful name for the function that it performs.

Think about automated bill paying as a real world example of the concepts of macro programming. When you enroll in an automated bill paying plan, you no longer write checks each month to pay recurring bills like the mortgage, the utilities, the telephone, and so on. Without automated bill paying, it takes a certain amount of time each month for you to write checks to pay those recurring bills. The time that it takes to initiate the automated bill paying plan is likely longer in the month that you set it up than if you just wrote the checks for the monthly bills. But, once you have the automated bill paying plan established (and perhaps allowing the bank a little debugging time!), the amount of time you spend each month dealing with those recurring bills is reduced. You instruct your bank how to handle those recurring bills. In turn they, in effect, write all those checks for you.

That's what macro programming can do for you. Instead of editing the program each time parameters change (for example, same analysis program, different data set), you write a SAS program that contains macro language statements. These macro language statements instruct the macro processor how to make those code changes for you. Then, when you run the program again, the only changes you make are to the values that the macro language uses to edit your program. Like directing the bank to add the water department to your automatic payment plan.

Example: Macro Programming Using Macro Variables

Consider another illustration of macro programming, this time including a sample program. The data set that is analyzed here is used throughout this book. The data represent computer book sales at a fictitious bookstore.

The following program is a monthly sales report for the computer section of the bookstore. If you were not using macro facility features, you would have to change the program every month at every location where the month value was referenced. You would also have to change the program once a year at every location where the year value was referenced.

Rather than doing these multiple edits, you can create macro variables at the beginning of the program that are set to the month and the year of interest, and place references to these macro variables throughout the program where they are needed. When you get ready to submit the program, the only changes you make are to the values of the macro variables. After you submit the program, the macro processor looks up the values of month and year that you set and substitutes those values as specified by your macro variable references.

In summary, you don't edit the DATA step and the PROC steps; you only change the values of the macro variables at the beginning of the program. The report layout stays the same, but the results are based on a different subset of the data set.

Don't worry about understanding the macro language coding at this point. Just realize that you can reuse the same program with different parameters to analyze a different subset of the data set. Macro language statements start with a percent sign (%). Macro variable references start with an ampersand (&). Both features are highlighted in the following code.

```
%let repmonth=4;
%let repyear=1998;
%let repmword=%sysfunc(mdy(&repmonth,1,&repyear),monname9.);

data month&repmonth;
   set books.ytdsales;
   mosale=month(datesold);
   label mosale='Month of Sale';
run;
proc tabulate data=month&repmonth;
   title "Sales During &repmword &repyear";
   where mosale=&repmonth and year(datesold)=&repyear;
   class section;
   var salepric listpric cost;
   tables section all='**TOTAL**',
          (salepric listpric cost)*(n*f=4. sum*f=dollar9.2);
run;

proc gchart data=month&repmonth
            (where=(mosale < %eval(&repmonth+1) and
                    year(datesold)=&repyear));
   title "Sales Through &repmword &repyear";
   pie section / coutline=black percent=arrow
                 sumvar=salepric noheading ;
run;

quit;
```

The output for this program is in Figure 1.2.

Figure 1.2   Output for sample program illustrating SAS macro programming

```
                   Sales During April 1998                         1

    ---------------------------------------------------------------
    |               |  Sale Price   |  List Price   |Wholesale Cost|
    |               |-------------+-------------+-------------|
    |               | N |   SUM     | N |   SUM     | N  |   SUM    |
    |-------------+----+---------+----+---------+----+---------|
    |Section        |    |         |    |         |    |         |
    |-------------|    |         |    |         |    |         |
    |Internet       | 145| $4579.71| 145| $4680.75| 145| $3318.77|
    |-------------+----+---------+----+---------+----+---------|
    |Networks and   |    |         |    |         |    |         |
    |Communication  |  55| $1633.01|  55| $1665.25|  55| $1177.46|
    |-------------+----+---------+----+---------+----+---------|
    |Operating      |    |         |    |         |    |         |
    |Systems        | 132| $4016.45| 132| $4108.40| 132| $2916.03|
    |-------------+----+---------+----+---------+----+---------|
    |Programming    |    |         |    |         |    |         |
    |Languages      |  60| $1835.07|  60| $1878.00|  60| $1330.98|
    |-------------+----+---------+----+---------+----+---------|
    |Web Design     | 131| $4015.50| 131| $4114.45| 131| $2910.87|
    |-------------+----+---------+----+---------+----+---------|
    |**TOTAL**      | 523|$16079.74| 523|$16446.85| 523|$11654.09|
    ---------------------------------------------------------------
```

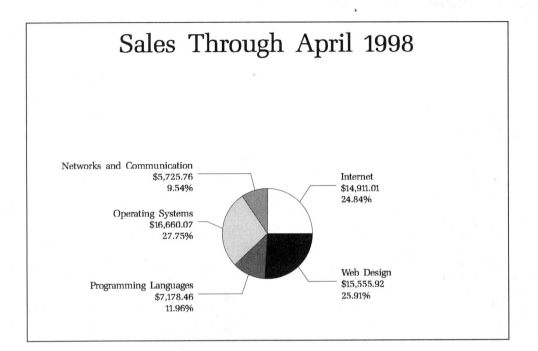

Changing just the first line of the program from

```
%let repmonth=4;
```

to

```
%let repmonth=5;
```

runs the same program, but now processes the data collected for May. No other editing of the program is required to process this subset. The output for May is shown in Figure 1.3.

Figure 1.3   Output for revised sample program

```
                        Sales During May 1998                       1

     --------------------------------------------------------------------
     |               | Sale Price    | List Price    |Wholesale Cost|
     |               |-------------+-------------+-------------|
     |               | N  |  SUM    | N  |  SUM    | N  |  SUM    |
     |-------------+----+---------+----+---------+----+---------|
     |Section        |    |         |    |         |    |         |
     |-------------|    |         |    |         |    |         |
     |Internet       | 190| $5803.11| 190| $5949.50| 190| $4213.08|
     |-------------+----+---------+----+---------+----+---------|
     |Networks and   |    |         |    |         |    |         |
     |Communication  |  60| $1763.37|  60| $1805.00|  60| $1280.48|
     |-------------+----+---------+----+---------+----+---------|
     |Operating      |    |         |    |         |    |         |
     |Systems        | 165| $5026.63| 165| $5132.75| 165| $3633.16|
     |-------------+----+---------+----+---------+----+---------|
     |Programming    |    |         |    |         |    |         |
     |Languages      |  90| $2666.00|  90| $2727.50|  90| $1931.61|
     |-------------+----+---------+----+---------+----+---------|
     |Web Design     | 135| $4149.40| 135| $4241.25| 135| $3000.62|
     |-------------+----+---------+----+---------+----+---------|
     |**TOTAL**      | 640|$19408.52| 640|$19856.00| 640|$14058.95|
     --------------------------------------------------------------------
```

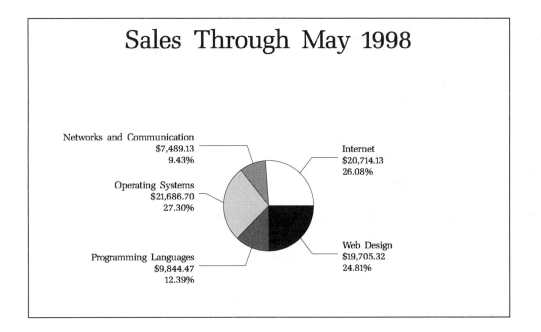

Where Can the SAS Macro Facility Be Used?

The macro facility can be used with all SAS products. We've seen in the monthly sales report an example of macro programming in base SAS.

Table 1.1 lists some SAS products and possible macro facility applications you can create. It also lists existing macro applications that come with the SAS product.

Table 1.1   SAS Macro Facility applications

SAS Product	Typical Applications of the Macro Facility
Base SAS	Customizes data set processing
	Customizes PROC steps
	Customizes reports
	Passes data between steps in a program
	Conditionally executes DATA steps and PROC steps
	Iteratively processes DATA steps and PROC steps
	Contains libraries of macro routines for working with macro variables
SAS Component Language*	Communicates between SAS program steps and SCL programs
	Communicates between SCL programs
SAS/CONNECT	Passes information between local and remote SAS sessions
SAS/GRAPH	Contains libraries of macro routines for annotating SAS/GRAPH output
SAS/IntrNet	Contains libraries of macro programs for formatting SAS output for web pages
SAS/TOOLKIT	Creates functions that can be used with the macro facility

*Note: For Version 7 of the SAS System, Screen Control Language is referred to as SAS Component Language, and it is abbreviated throughout this book as SCL.

Examples of the SAS Macro Facility

The following examples of the SAS macro facility illustrate some of the tasks that the macro processor can perform for you. There's no need to understand the coding of these programs at this point (although the code is included and may be useful to you later). What you should gain from this section is an idea of the kinds of SAS programming tasks that can be delegated to the macro processor.

Example: Displaying SAS System Information with Macro Variables Automatically Defined by the SAS System

The SAS System comes with a set of automatic macro variables that you can reference in your SAS programs. Most of these macro variables deal with system-related items like date, time, operating system, and version of SAS. Using these automatically defined macro variables is the simplest application of the macro facility. The following example incorporates some of these automatic macro variables. Note that the automatic macro variable names are preceded by ampersands. Assume the report was run on May 31, 1998. The report shows sales for 1998 through May 31.

```
title "Sales Report";
title2 "As of &systime &sysday &sysdate";
title3 "Using SAS Version: &sysver";
proc means data=books.ytdsales n sum;
  var salepric;
run;
```

The output for this program is in Figure 1.4.

Figure 1.4   Output for program using automatically defined SAS macro variables

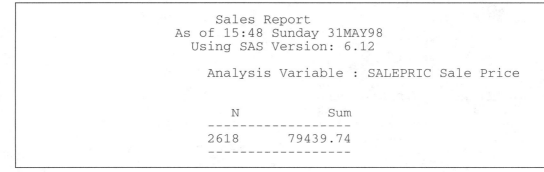

```
                        Sales Report
                As of 15:48 Sunday 31MAY98
                 Using SAS Version: 6.12

            Analysis Variable : SALEPRIC Sale Price


               N                Sum
          ------------------
           2618          79439.74
          ------------------
```

Example: Substituting Information Multiple Times

The example that started on page 5 demonstrated reuse of the same program by simply changing the values of the macro variables at the beginning of the program. A new subset of data is analyzed each time the values of the macro variables are changed.

It is relatively simple to create and reference these macro variables. Besides being able to reuse your program code, the advantages in using macro variables include reducing coding time and reducing programming errors by not having to manage so many lines of code.

Example: Conditional Processing of DATA Steps and PROC Steps

Macro programs can use macro variables and macro programming statements to select the steps and the SAS language statements executed in a SAS program. These conditional processing macro language statements are similar in syntax and structure to SAS language statements.

There are two PROC steps in the macro program below. The first PROC MEANS step runs daily. The second PROC MEANS step runs only on Fridays. The conditional macro language statements direct the macro processor to run the second PROC step only on Fridays. Assume the program was run on Friday, August 21, 1998.

Macro language statements start with percent signs and macro variable references start with ampersands.

```
%macro daily;
   proc means data=books.ytdsales(where=(datesold=today()))
                  maxdec=2 sum;
     title "Daily Sales Report for &sysdate";
     class section;
     var salepric;
   run;
%if &sysday=Friday %then %do;
     proc means data=books.ytdsales
            (where=(today()-6 le datesold le today()))
            sum maxdec=2;
        title "Weekly Sales Report Week Ending &sysdate";
        class section;
        var salepric;
     run;
%end;
%mend daily;

%daily
```

The output for this program is in Figure 1.5.

**Figure 1.5   Output for sample program that uses conditional macro language
statements**

```
                  Daily Sales Report for 21AUG98

         Analysis Variable : SALEPRIC Sale Price


         SECTION                        N Obs           Sum
         ---------------------------------------------------
         Internet                         6          176.70

         Networks and Communication       2           65.90

         Operating Systems                5          134.75

         Programming Languages            1           24.95

         Web Design                       3           85.85
         ---------------------------------------------------


           Weekly Sales Report Week Ending 21AUG98

         Analysis Variable : SALEPRIC Sale Price


         SECTION                        N Obs           Sum
         ---------------------------------------------------
         Internet                        38         1112.33

         Networks and Communication       7          236.76

         Operating Systems               33         1055.58

         Programming Languages           11          326.45

         Web Design                      41         1248.99
```

Example: Iterative Processing

Coding each iteration of a programming process that contains multiple iterations is a lengthy task. The %DO loops in the macro language can take over some of that iterative coding for you. A macro program can build the code for each iteration of a repetitive programming process based on the specifications of the %DO loop.

As an illustration of iterative processing, the following macro program creates 12 data sets, one for each month of the year. Without macro programming, you would have to enter the 12 data set names in the DATA statement and enter all the ELSE statements that direct observations to the right data set. A macro language %DO loop can build those statements for you.

```
%macro makesets;
   data
     %do i=1 %to 12;
        month&i
     %end;
     ;
     set books.ytdsales;
     mosale=month(datesold);
     if mosale=1 then output month1;
     %do i=2 %to 12;
        else if mosale=&i then output month&i;
     %end;
   run;
%mend makesets;

%makesets
```

After interpretation by the macro processor, the program becomes:

```
data month1 month2 month3 month4 month5 month6
     month7 month8 month9 month10 month11 month12
     ;
   set books.ytdsales;
   mosale=month(datesold);
   if mosale=1 then output month1;
   else if mosale=2 then output month2;
   else if mosale=3 then output month3;
   else if mosale=4 then output month4;
   else if mosale=5 then output month5;
   else if mosale=6 then output month6;
   else if mosale=7 then output month7;
   else if mosale=8 then output month8;
   else if mosale=9 then output month9;
   else if mosale=10 then output month10;
   else if mosale=11 then output month11;
   else if mosale=12 then output month12;
   run;
```

Macro language statements built the SAS language DATA statement and all of the DATA step ELSE statements for you.

A few macro programming statements direct the macro processor to build the complete DATA step for you. By doing this, you avoid the tedious task of entering all the data set names and all those ELSE statements. Repetitive coding tasks are a breeding ground for bugs in your programs. Thus, turning these tasks over to the macro processor may reduce the number of errors in your SAS programs.

Example: Passing Information between Program Steps

The macro facility can act as a bridge between steps in your SAS programs. The SAS language functions that interact with the macro facility can transfer information between steps in your SAS programs.

The program below calculates total sales for two sections in the computer department of the bookstore. That value is then inserted in the TITLE statement of the PROC GCHART output. The SYMPUT SAS language routine instructs the macro processor to hold on to the total sales value after the DATA step finishes. The total sales value is then available to subsequent steps in the program.

The output for the following program is in Figure 1.6.

```
data temp;
   set books.ytdsales end=lastobs;
   retain sumintwb 0;
   if section in ('Internet','Web Design') then
     sumintwb=sumintwb + salepric;
   if lastobs then
     call symput('INTWEBSL',put(sumintwb,dollar10.2));
run;
proc gchart data=temp;
   title "Internet and Web Design Sales: &intwebsl";
   title2 "As of &enddate";
   hbar section / sumvar=salepric;
   format salepric dollar10.2;
run;

quit;
```

Figure 1.6   Output for program that passes data from a DATA step to a PROC step

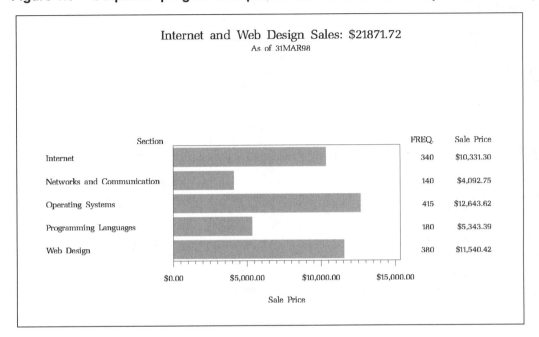

Without the SYMPUT routine, you have to submit two programs. The first SAS program calculates the total sales for the two sections. After the first program ends, you find the total sales value in the output. Then you have to edit the second program and update the TITLE statement with the total sales value that you copied from the output of the first program.

Example: Interface to SAS Language Functions

The SAS language has libraries of functions that can be used in your macro language programs. Some uses of these functions include incorporating information about a data set in a title, checking the existence of a data set, and finding the number of observations in a data set.

In the following macro language program, a report is produced for a specified data set. The data set name is passed as a parameter to the macro program. The macro program determines the number of observations in the data set and the date that the data set was created. This information is inserted in the title. PROC MEANS then produces descriptive statistics.

```
%macro dsreport(dsname);
   title "Report on Data Set &dsname";
```

```
%let dsid=%sysfunc(open(&dsname));

%*----How many obs are in the data set?;
%let nobs=%sysfunc(attrn(&dsid,nobs));

%*----When was the data set created?;
%let when = %sysfunc(putn(
            %sysfunc(attrn(&dsid,crdte)),datetime9.));

title2 "Num Obs: &nobs    Date Created: &when";

proc means data=&dsname sum maxdec=2;
   class section;
   var salepric;
run;
%mend dsreport;

%dsreport(books.ytdsales)
```

The output for the above program is in Figure 1.7.

Figure 1.7   Output for macro program using SAS language functions

```
                Report on Data Set books.ytdsales
              Num Obs: 3489    Date Created: 15JUL98

           Analysis Variable : SALEPRIC Sale Price


           SECTION                      N Obs            Sum
           ------------------------------------------------
           Internet                       904        27619.62

           Networks and Communication     332         9869.86

           Operating Systems              950        28833.04

           Programming Languages          452        13445.51

           Web Design                     851        25973.70
           ------------------------------------------------
```

Example: SAS Component Language Programs and the Macro Facility

The macro facility can be used in SAS Component Language (SCL) programs to update SAS/AF screens, pass data between SCL programs, and pass data between SCL programs and SAS language programs.

In the following example, a SUBMIT block encloses a PROC FREQ step. The results of the PROC FREQ step are moved to macro variables using SAS language functions in a DATA step. The macro variables are also accessible to the SCL program. The SCL program obtains the values from the macro variables and then displays them on the SAS/AF screen. NWEB and NNET are SCL fields on the SAS/AF screen.

```
runrep:
   submit continue;
      proc freq data=books.ytdsales;
         tables section / out=freqs noprint;
      run;
      data _null_;
         set freqs;
         if section='Web Design' then
                 call symput("WEBDESGN",count);
         else if section='Internet' then
                 call symput("INTERNET",count);
      run;
   endsubmit;

   *----Update screen;
   nweb=symget("WEBDESGN");
   nnet=symget("INTERNET");
return;
```

Figure 1.8 shows an example of the above program. When the "Internet/Web Design" button is selected, the report runs, the macro variables are created, and the screen fields are updated.

Figure 1.8   Sample SAS/AF screen using a program that creates macro variables to update SAS/AF screen fields

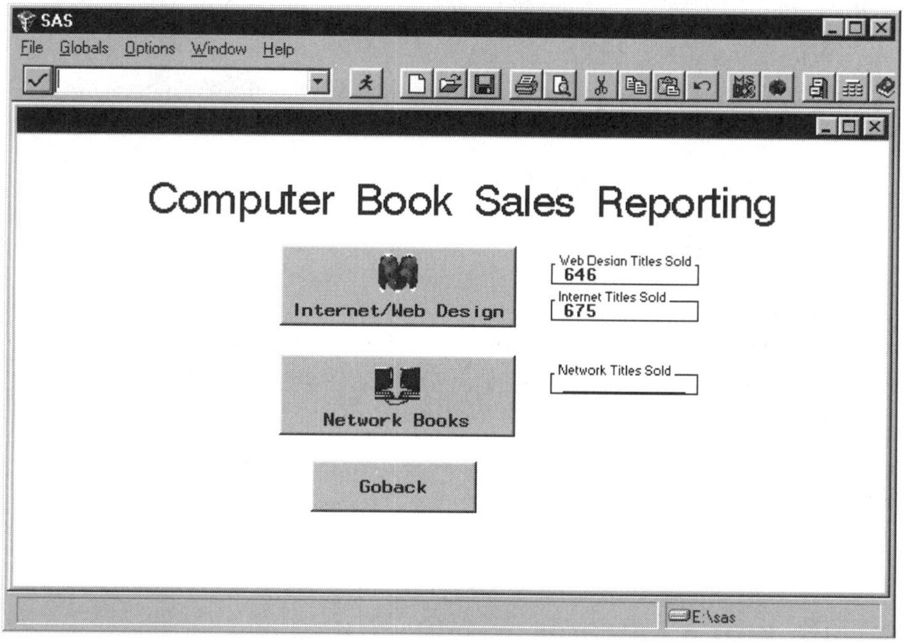

How Can This Book Help You Understand the SAS Macro Facility?

This book is for beginning through experienced users of the SAS macro facility. It shows you how to delegate some of your SAS programming tasks to the macro facility.

This book assumes you have beginner to intermediate experience writing SAS language programs. SAS language and SAS programming concepts are not reviewed.

This book is less inclusive and spends less time on reference details than *SAS Macro Language: Reference*. Rather, the focus is on making the macro facility a tool you can use.

The technical aspects of macro processing are described in this book. While understanding the technical aspects is not necessary to begin to reap the benefits of the SAS macro facility, this knowledge may help you more wisely apply macro programming techniques.

Don't worry if the technical aspects are difficult to grasp at first. Instead, jump in and start using the simpler features of the macro facility. Try macro variables first. You're bound to make some errors, but those errors help you understand macro processing. Eventually, as your macro programming skills improve, a more thorough understanding of macro processing can reduce the number of macro programming errors you make and make it easier to debug your programs.

This book starts with the easier features of the SAS macro facility. These features are building blocks for the later topics. The features of the macro facility are interrelated, and so occasionally you may see some features used before they are formally discussed.

Because macro facility features are interrelated, this book does not have to be read in a linear fashion. Work through sections as appropriate for your needs. Return to earlier sections when that information becomes pertinent. However, it is best to start with the technical information in Chapter 2 and move on to the macro variable chapter, Chapter 3. You might then work with macro variables extensively and try some of the features like macro functions and macro expressions that are described in Chapter 6. After gaining confidence in how macro variables work, you might try writing macro programs. You can learn how to do this in Chapter 4 and then try using the macro programming statements in Chapter 6.

You may find it useful to learn about macro facility interfaces before you cover macro programs. Chapter 7 includes information useful for SCL programmers, PROC SQL programmers, and DATA step programmers.

About the Data and Programs in this Book

The examples in this book are illustrated with sales data from a fictitious bookstore. The DATA step to create this data set is in Appendix C. A PROC CONTENTS listing for this data set is also in Appendix C.

The examples and screens in this book were produced using Release 6.12 of SAS under Windows 95. Where appropriate, information about Version 7 features is included.

The Typographical Styles in This Book

The following styles have special meaning when describing the syntax of macro language statements and SAS language statements in this book.

- Values in *italics* identify arguments and values that you supply.

- Arguments enclosed in angle brackets (< >) are optional.

- Arguments separated with a vertical bar (|) indicate mutually exclusive choices.

For example, the syntax of the %SYSEVALF function is written as follows:

```
%SYSEVALF(arithmetic expression|logical expression
    <,conversion-type>)
```

When specifying the %SYSEVALF function, you must specify either an arithmetic expression or a logical expression. Specifying a conversion type is optional.

CHAPTER 2

Mechanics of Macro Processing

Understanding the steps that the SAS System takes to process a program will help you determine where macro facility features can be incorporated in your SAS programs. You do not need a detailed knowledge of the mechanics of macro processing to write SAS programs that include macro features. However, an understanding of the timing of macro language processing as it relates to SAS language processing can help you write more powerful programs and make it easier for you to debug programs that contain macro features.

The examples in Chapter 1 showed you how you can enhance your SAS programming with the macro facility. These examples help to illustrate when and how the macro processor does its work.

There are just a few basic concepts in macro processing to add to your knowledge of SAS processing. If you already know how SAS programs are compiled and executed, you are well on your way to understanding the mechanics of macro processing.

As you read through this chapter, keep in mind that the macro processor is your SAS programming assistant, helping you code your SAS programs.

The Vocabulary of SAS Processing

In this chapter, several terms are used to describe SAS processing. These terms are reviewed in Table 2.1.

Table 2.1   Terms commonly used to describe SAS processing

Term	Description
input stack	Holds a SAS program after it has been submitted and while it waits for processing by the word scanner.
word scanner	Scans the commands it takes from the input stack and breaks the commands into tokens. Determines the destination of the token: DATA step compiler, macro processor, etc.
token	Fundamental unit in the SAS language. SAS commands must be broken down into tokens, or tokenized, before the commands can be compiled. Tokens are the actual words in the SAS statements as well as the literal strings, numbers, and symbols.
compiler	Checks the syntax of tokens received from the word scanner. After completing syntax checking, the compiler translates the tokens into a form for execution.
macro processor	Processes macro language references and statements.
macro trigger	The symbols & and %, when followed by a letter or underscore, that signal the word scanner to transfer what follows to the macro processor.
macro symbol table	The area in the macro processor where macro variables and their associated values are stored.

SAS Processing without Macro Activity

SAS programs can be submitted for processing from several locations including:

- an interactive SAS session from the display manager Program Editor

- a batch program

- a noninteractive program submission

- the display manager command line

- an SCL SUBMIT block

- the SCL Compile command.

In all cases, submitted SAS programs start out in the input stack. The word scanner takes statements from the input stack and tokenizes the statements into words and symbols. The word scanner's job is to then direct the tokens to the right location. The word scanner may direct tokens to the DATA step compiler, the macro processor, the command processor, or the SCL compiler. The compiler or processor that receives the tokens checks for syntax errors. If none are found, the step is executed.

The processing of a SAS program that contains no macro facility features is illustrated in Figure 2.1.

Figure 2.1   Basic processing of a SAS program

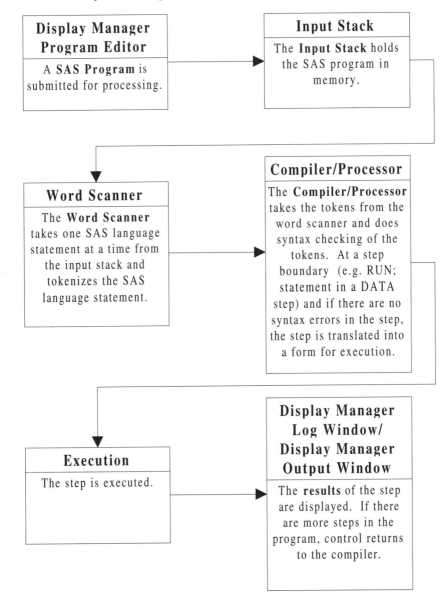

Understanding Tokens

The fundamental building blocks of a SAS program are the tokens that the word scanner creates from your SAS language statements. Each word, literal string, number, and special symbol in the statements in your program is a token.

The word scanner determines that a token ends when either a blank is found following a token or when another token begins. The maximum length of a token under Version 6 is 200 characters. Under Version 7, the maximum length of a token is 32767 characters.

Two special symbol tokens, when followed by either a letter or underscore, signal the word scanner to turn processing over to the macro processor. These two characters, the ampersand (&) and the percent sign (%), are called macro triggers.

The four types of tokens that the SAS System recognizes are described in Table 2.2.

Table 2.2   The types of tokens that the SAS System recognizes

Type of Token	Description	Examples
literal	A string of characters enclosed in single or double quotation marks.	'My program text' "My program text"
numbers	A string of digits including integers, decimal values, and exponential notation. Dates, times, and hexadecimal constants are also number tokens.	123456 '30APR1999'D 9 8 . 7 6 5 4 3. '01'x 6.023E23
names	The "words" in your programs. Name tokens are strings of characters beginning with a letter or underscore and continuing with letters, underscores, or digits. Periods can be part of a name token when referring to a format.	proc _n_ ssn. if mmddyy8. Descending var1 var2 var3 var4 var5
special	Characters other than a letter, number, or underscore that have a special meaning to the SAS System.	; + - * / ** () {} & %

The importance of understanding tokenization is evident if you have ever dealt with unmatched quotation marks in your SAS language statements. Matched quotation marks delimit a literal token. When a closing quotation mark is omitted, the SAS System continues to add text to your literal token beyond what you intended. The SAS programming statements added to the literal token never get tokenized by the word scanner. Eventually, the literal token terminates when either another quotation mark is encountered or the literal token reaches its maximum length (200 characters under Version 6 and 32K characters under Version 7). At that point, your program cannot compile correctly and processing stops.

Tokenizing a SAS Program

The next figures illustrate the tokenization of a DATA step. In Figure 2.2, the program has been submitted and is waiting in the input stack for tokenization by the word scanner.

Figure 2.2   A SAS program has been submitted and waits in the input stack for tokenization

```
Input Stack

data web;
  set books.ytdsales;
  if section="Web Design";
run;
```

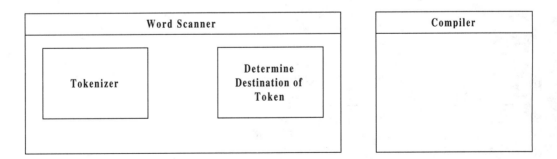

In Figure 2.3 the word scanner tokenizes the program and determines the destination of the tokens. In this example, the word scanner sends the tokens to the DATA step compiler.

Figure 2.3 The word scanner tokenizes the SAS language statements in the program

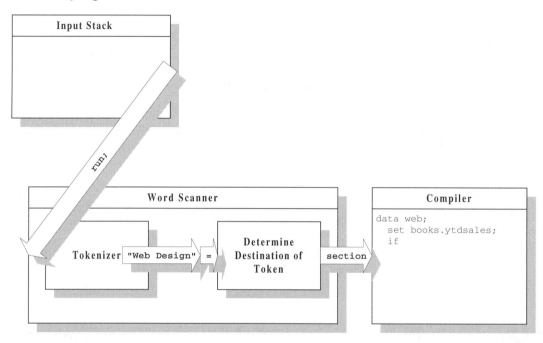

When the compiler receives the semicolon following the RUN statement, it stops taking tokens from the word scanner. The compiler looks for syntax errors. If no errors are found, the step is compiled and executed.

Comparing Macro Language Processing and SAS Language Processing

It is important to realize that there are differences between the SAS language and the SAS macro language. You are probably familiar with terms like variables and statements in the SAS language. The macro language also has variables and statements, but these variables and statements are different from those in the SAS language and serve different purposes.

The main function of the macro facility is to help you build SAS language statements that can be tokenized, compiled, and executed. By taking over some of your coding tasks, the macro processor shortens the amount of coding you do.

Recall that all SAS programs are compiled and executed the same way. After a SAS program is submitted, the statements wait in the input stack for processing. The word scanner then takes each SAS language statement from the input stack and tokenizes it. The compiler requests the tokens, does syntax checking, and at a step boundary passes the compiled statements on for execution.

When the word scanner detects a macro trigger followed by a name token, it sends what follows to the macro processor and temporarily turns processing over to the macro processor. The word scanner suspends tokenization while the macro processor completes its job. Therefore, processing of a macro language reference occurs *after* tokenization and *before* compilation.

As your SAS programming assistant, the macro processor codes SAS language statements for you based on the guidelines you give it. The way you communicate your requests to the macro processor is through the macro language. The macro processor takes the macro language statements you write and turns them into SAS language statements. The macro processor puts the SAS language statements that it builds back on top of the input stack. The word scanner then resumes its work by tokenizing the newly built SAS language statements that have come from the macro processor.

Processing a SAS Program that Contains Macro Language

This section describes how a SAS program that includes macro language statements is processed. The macro processor starts working when the word scanner encounters a macro trigger followed by a letter or underscore. The word scanner then directs the results of its tokenization to the macro processor. Tokens are sent to the macro processor until the macro reference is terminated. The macro processor resolves macro language references and returns the results to top of the input stack. The word scanner then resumes tokenization. Figure 2.4 illustrates this process.

Figure 2.4   SAS processing when macro facility features are included in the program

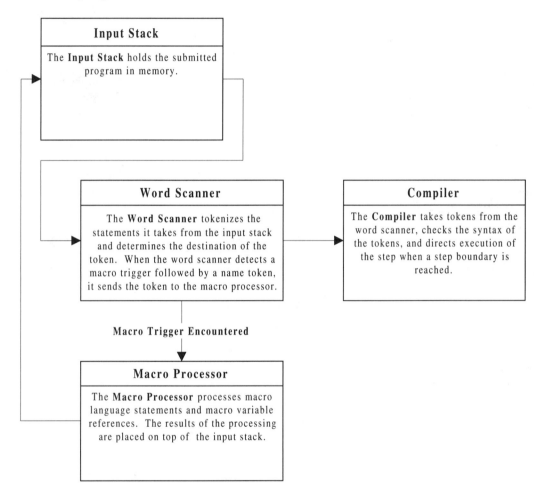

The next several figures illustrate the above process with the program from Figure 2.2. This program now contains one macro language statement and one macro variable reference.

The %LET macro language statement assigns a value to a macro variable. The %LET statement tells the macro processor to store the macro variable name and its associated text in the macro symbol table.

The macro variable is referenced in the DATA step where the text associated with the macro variable should be substituted. The ampersand token followed by a name token is the instruction to the macro processor to look in the macro symbol table for the text associated with the macro variable whose name follows the ampersand. At the location of the macro variable reference in the DATA step, the macro processor replaces the reference with the macro variable's value.

The value of the macro variable REPGRP in the program in the next several figures is used to define a subset of the data set. In this example, only observations from the section "Web Design" are written to the output data set.

The value of the macro variable is stored in the macro symbol table for the duration of the SAS session. When a SAS session starts, the SAS System automatically defines several macro variables. These automatic macro variables are also stored in the macro symbol table. A few of the automatic macro variables are shown in the figures.

In Figure 2.5, the program has been submitted.

Figure 2.5   The program with macro facility features has been submitted and the word scanner is ready to tokenize

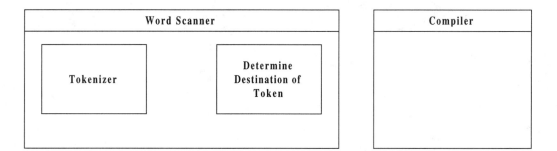

Figure 2.6 shows how a macro language statement is taken from the input stack, tokenized by the word scanner, and passed to the macro processor.

Figure 2.6   A macro language statement is processed

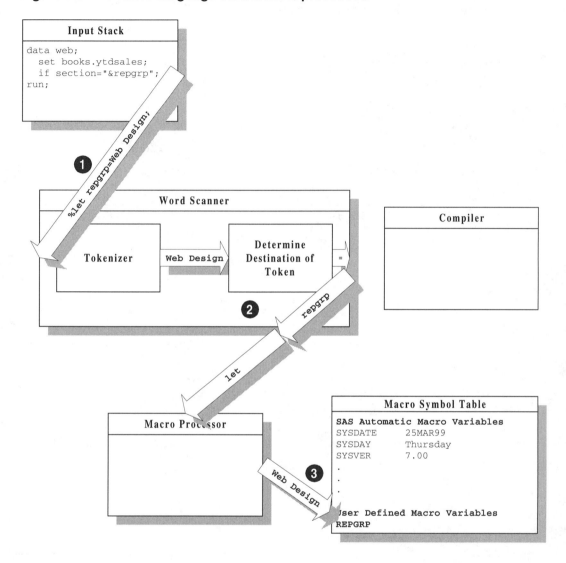

The three steps in Figure 2.6 are

1 Statements are taken from the input stack one at a time. The %LET statement is the first one to be processed by the word scanner.

2 When the word scanner detects a percent sign (%) followed by the word LET, this macro trigger tells the word scanner to direct the tokens that follow to the macro processor. The macro processor stops processing the tokens when the semicolon (;) terminating the %LET statement is encountered.

3 Last, the macro processor places the macro variable REPGRP and its associated text, *Web Design*, in the macro symbol table.

No quotation marks enclose the literal token *Web Design*. This is one way in which the macro language is different from the SAS language. Macro variable values are always text; quotation marks are not needed to indicate text constants in the macro language.

The word scanner continues to tokenize the program. It now encounters the macro variable reference to REPGRP and directs resolution of this reference to the macro processor. This is shown in Figure 2.7. A description of the three steps in Figure 2.7 follows.

Figure 2.7   The macro variable reference &REPGRP is resolved by the macro processor

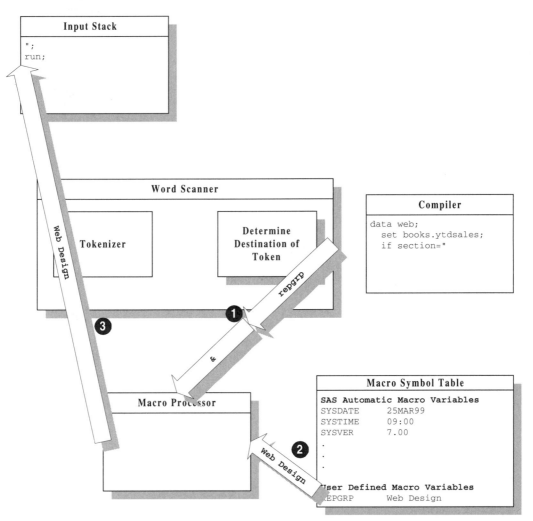

❶ When the word scanner encounters the ampersand followed by REPGRP, it directs processing to the macro processor.

❷ The macro processor looks up the macro variable REPGRP and takes its value from the macro symbol table.

❸ The macro processor places the value of the macro variable REPGRP on top of the input stack.

The value of the macro variable REPGRP is now on top of the input stack in Figure 2.8. Remember that the macro variable reference was enclosed in double quotes. Therefore, the value of the macro variable is one literal token.

Figure 2.8   The value of macro variable REPGRP is on top of the input stack

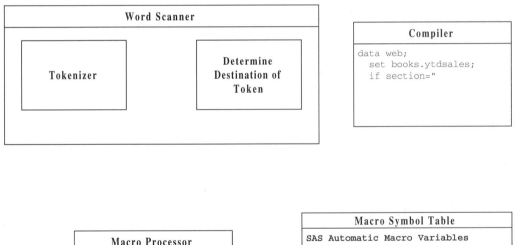

Next, the value of the macro variable is transferred from the input stack to the word scanner. This is shown in Figure 2.9.

Figure 2.9   The value of the macro variable REPGRP is transferred to the word scanner

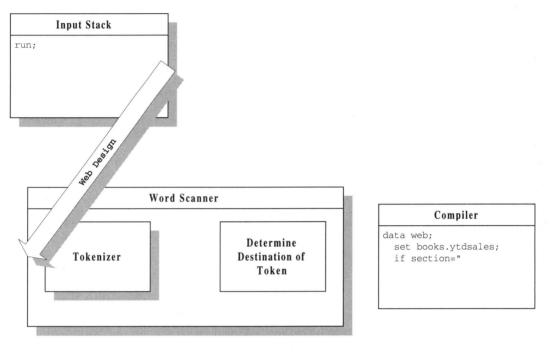

The value of the macro variable REPGRP passes through the word scanner as a literal token and is transferred to the compiler. Now the last statement in the DATA step is sent to the word scanner as shown in Figure 2.10.

Figure 2.10 The compiler receives the value of the macro variable REPGRP and the last statement in the DATA step is sent to the word scanner

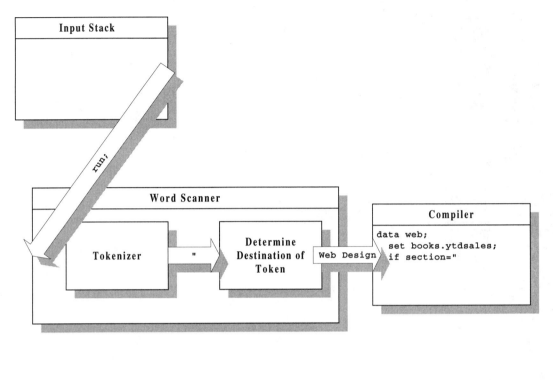

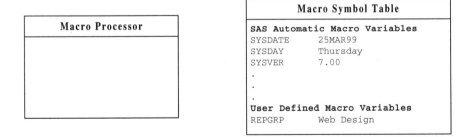

Finally, the RUN statement terminating the DATA step is sent to the compiler and the compiler compiles the step. This is shown in Figure 2.11.

Figure 2.11 The RUN statement is transferred to the compiler and the step is compiled

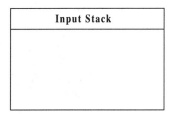

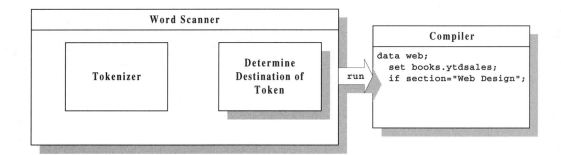

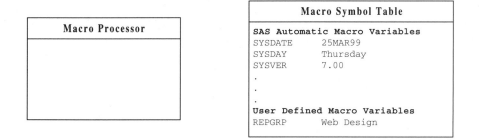

In conclusion, when you are writing SAS programs that include macro facility features, remember the distinction between when SAS language is processed and when macro language is processed. Macro language builds SAS language. Macro language is resolved before SAS language is compiled and executed.

CHAPTER 3

Macro Variables

Macro variables are the most fundamental part of the SAS macro facility. They are the tools to use to begin writing reusable programs. There is relatively little to learn and yet there is great potential in the application of macro variables.

This chapter describes how to define and use SAS macro variables as symbols for text substitution. Before you finish this chapter, you will write programs that contain macro variables. Programming with macro variables will give you an appreciation of the timing of macro processing and provide you with a foundation for understanding the features described later in this book.

Basic Concepts of Macro Variables

There are many features of macro variables. The following list describes the basic characteristics of macro variables.

- **A macro variable can be referenced anywhere in a SAS program other than in data lines.**
  When the macro processor encounters the reference, the value assigned to the macro variable is substituted in the reference's place. Macro variables can modify SAS language statements in DATA steps, PROC steps, and SCL programs.

- **Macro variables can be used in open code as well as in macro programs.**
  When macro variables are used outside of macro programs, they are in open code. Macro programs are described in the next chapter. The examples in this chapter only deal with macro variables in open code.

- **Macro variables can be created by the SAS System and by your programs.**
  There are two types of macro variables: automatic macro variables and user-defined macro variables. Automatic macro variables are defined by the SAS System each time a SAS session is started and they remain available for you to use throughout your SAS session. Most automatic macro variables contain information about your SAS session: time of day that the session was invoked, version of SAS, etc. Most automatic macro variable values remain constant throughout your SAS session and most cannot be modified by you.

  User-defined macro variables are defined by you for your own applications. They can be defined anywhere in your SAS program other than in data lines.

- **Macro variables can be stored in either the global symbol table or in a local symbol table.**
  When a macro variable is created, the macro processor adds the macro variable to a macro symbol table. There are two types of macro symbol tables: global and local.

  Macro variables created in open code reside in the global symbol table. A macro variable created in a macro program can reside either in a macro symbol table local to that macro program or in the global symbol table. Since the examples in this chapter deal with macro variables created in open code, these macro variables reside in the global symbol table.

  The value that you assign to a macro variable stored in the global symbol table stays the same throughout the SAS session unless you change it. Automatic macro variables are stored in the global symbol table.

  The value assigned to a macro variable created in a macro program and defined as local to a macro program stays the same throughout execution of the macro program unless you change it. A local macro variable is deleted when the macro program that created it ends.

- **Macro variable values are text values**.
  All values assigned to macro variables are considered text values. This includes numbers. When you want to do calculations with macro variables, you must tell the macro processor to treat the values as numbers. The result of a calculation is considered a text value.

  The case of the character value assigned to a macro variable is preserved. That is, a value in lowercase remains lowercase, uppercase remains uppercase, and mixed case remains mixed case.

Leading and trailing blanks are removed from the macro variable value before the value is placed in the macro symbol table.

The maximum length of text that can be assigned to a macro variable value in Version 6 of the SAS System is 32K characters; in Version 7, the maximum length is 64K. The minimum length is 0 characters. You do not have to declare the length of a macro variable; its length is determined each time a value is assigned.

- **The name assigned to a macro variable must be a valid SAS name.**
  A macro variable name can be up to eight characters in length in Version 6 and up to 32 characters in Version 7. The macro variable name must start with a letter or underscore, and continue with either letters, numbers, or underscores.

- **Macro variables are not data set variables and they have a different purpose from data set variables.**
  Macro variables help you build your SAS programs and do not directly relate to observations in a data set. A macro variable only has one value while a data set variable can have multiple values, one for each observation in a data set.

Referencing Macro Variables

A macro variable is referenced in your program by preceding the macro variable name with an ampersand (&). In the following program, two macro variables are created in open code by using the %LET statement. (The %LET statement is described in more detail later in this chapter.) These two variables are then referenced in the program. An automatic macro variable that was defined by the SAS System at the start of the SAS session is also referenced.

Note the double quotation marks around the text on the TITLE statement. When referencing macro variables in a SAS statement, double quotation marks allow resolution of macro variable references; single quotation marks do not. Use of quotation marks is described in the next section.

```
%let reptitle=Book Section;
%let reptvar=section;

title "Frequencies by &reptitle as of &sysday";
proc freq data=books.ytdsales;
   tables &reptvar;
run;
```

After the macro processor resolves the macro variable references and assuming the program was run on a Friday, the program now becomes:

```
title "Frequencies by Book Section as of Friday";
proc freq data=books.ytdsales;
  tables section;
run;
```

Since these macro variables were created in open code, they can be referenced anywhere in your program any number of times. The values of these macro variables remain the same throughout the program unless you change them. The following program adds a PROC MEANS step to the program above.

```
%let reptitle=Book Section;
%let reptvar=section;

title "Frequencies by &reptitle as of &sysday";
proc freq data=books.ytdsales;
 tables &reptvar;
run;

title "Means by &reptitle as of &sysday";
proc means data=books.ytdsales;
  class &reptvar;
  var salepric;
run;
```

The two user-defined macro variables were only defined once, but they were referenced more than once. After the macro processor resolves the macro variable references and assuming the program was run on a Friday, the program now becomes:

```
title "Frequencies by Book Section as of Friday";
proc freq data=books.ytdsales;
  tables section;
run;

title "Means by Book Section as of Friday";
proc means data=books.ytdsales;
  class section;
  var salepric;
run;
```

Understanding Macro Variable Resolution and the Use of Single and Double Quotation Marks

When you want a macro variable's value to be included as part of a literal string in the SAS language, you must enclose the string with double quotation marks. A macro variable reference enclosed within single quotation marks will not be resolved. The word scanner does not look for macro triggers in the characters between single quotation marks.

The first TITLE statement in the next program has text enclosed in double quotation marks. The macro variable references on that statement are resolved. The second TITLE statement has text enclosed in single quotation marks. The macro variable references on that statement are not resolved.

```
%let reptitle=Section;
%let reptvar=section;

title "Frequencies by &reptitle as of &sysday";
proc freq data=books.ytdsales;
   tables &reptvar;
run;

title 'Means by &reptitle as of &sysday';
proc means data=books.ytdsales sum maxdec=2;
   class &reptvar;
   var salepric;
run;
```

After the macro processor resolves the macro variable references and assuming the program was run on a Friday, the program now becomes:

```
title "Frequencies by Section as of Friday";
proc freq data=books.ytdsales;
   tables section;
run;

title 'Means by &reptitle as of &sysday';
proc means data=books.ytdsales sum maxdec=2;
   class section;
   var salepric; ·
run;
```

The macro variable references on the second TITLE statement are not sent to the macro processor for resolution. The references instead are treated as part of the text in the TITLE statement, and thus no warnings or error messages are displayed. The output for the PROC MEANS step is shown in Figure 3.1.

Figure 3.1   Output for PROC MEANS step with title enclosed in single quotation marks

```
                    Means by &reptitle as of &sysday

        Analysis Variable : SALEPRIC Sale Price


        SECTION                           N Obs            Sum
        ---------------------------------------------------------
        Internet                            340        8912.15

        Networks and Communication          140        4945.68

        Operating Systems                   415       12271.79

        Programming Languages               180        5574.27

        Web Design                          380       10845.36
        ---------------------------------------------------------
```

Displaying Macro Variable Values

Displaying macro variable values as the macro processor resolves them is very useful in showing you how and when the macro processor does its work. Further, this information can help you debug your programs.

Two ways to display macro variable values are with the macro language statement %PUT and with the SAS system option SYMBOLGEN. Both of these features write the values of macro variables to the SAS log.

Using the %PUT statement

The %PUT statement instructs the macro processor to write information to the SAS log. Text and macro variable values can be displayed with %PUT. The %PUT statement can be submitted by itself from the display manager Program Editor or from within a SAS program. Since %PUT is a macro language statement, it does not need to be part of a DATA step or PROC step. It only displays text and information about macro variables.

The %PUT statement is written as follows:

```
%put &macro-variable-name;
```

Three other ways the %PUT statement can be written are as follows:

```
%put _automatic_;
%put _user_;
%put _all_;
```

The statement %PUT _AUTOMATIC_ lists the values of all the automatic macro variables. %PUT _USER_ lists the values of all macro variables that the user has defined in the SAS session. %PUT _ALL_ lists both the automatic and user-defined macro variables. An excerpt of the SAS log after submitting %PUT _AUTOMATIC_ from the Program Editor of a Version 6 SAS session under Windows 95 looks like this:

```
AUTOMATIC AFDSID 0
AUTOMATIC AFDSNAME
AUTOMATIC AFLIB
AUTOMATIC AFSTR1
AUTOMATIC AFSTR2
AUTOMATIC FSPBDV
AUTOMATIC SYSBUFFR
AUTOMATIC SYSCMD
AUTOMATIC SYSDATE 24OCT97
AUTOMATIC SYSDAY Friday
AUTOMATIC SYSDEVIC
AUTOMATIC SYSDSN            _NULL_
AUTOMATIC SYSENV FORE
AUTOMATIC SYSERR 0
AUTOMATIC SYSFILRC 0
AUTOMATIC SYSINDEX 0
AUTOMATIC SYSINFO 0
AUTOMATIC SYSJOBID 4294779921
AUTOMATIC SYSLAST _NULL_
AUTOMATIC SYSLCKRC 0
AUTOMATIC SYSLIBRC 0
AUTOMATIC SYSMENV S
AUTOMATIC SYSMSG
AUTOMATIC SYSPARM
AUTOMATIC SYSPBUFF
AUTOMATIC SYSRC 0
AUTOMATIC SYSSCP WIN
AUTOMATIC SYSSCPL WIN_95
AUTOMATIC SYSSITE 0099999999
AUTOMATIC SYSTIME 14:48
AUTOMATIC SYSVER 6.12
AUTOMATIC SYSVLONG 6.12.0020P103196
```

Text added to %PUT statements can make the results more informative and easier to read. For example, three %PUT statements with text are added to the following program.

```
%let reptitle=Book Section;
%let reptvar=section;
```

```
%put My macro variable REPTITLE has the value &reptitle;
%put My macro variable REPTVAR has the value &reptvar;
%put The automatic macro variable sysday has the value &sysday;

title "Frequencies by &reptitle as of &sysday";
proc freq data=books.ytdsales;
  tables &reptvar;
run;
```

The SAS log of this program follows:

```
31    %let reptitle=Book Section;
32    %let reptvar=section;
33
34    %put My macro variable REPTITLE has the value &reptitle;
My macro variable REPTITLE has the value Book Section
35    %put My macro variable REPTVAR has the value &reptvar;
My macro variable REPTVAR has the value section
36    %put The automatic macro variable sysday has the value
&sysday;
The automatic macro variable sysday has the value Friday
37
38    title "Frequencies by &reptitle as of &sysday";
39    proc freq data=books.ytdsales;
40      tables &reptvar;
41    run;

NOTE: The PROCEDURE FREQ used 0.0 seconds.
```

Note that the values of the macro variables on the %PUT statements are displayed in the SAS Log window. The values of the same macro variables in the PROC FREQ step are not displayed as they are resolved. The next section describes how you can display in the SAS log the values of macro variables that are included in SAS language statements.

Enabling the SYMBOLGEN Option to Display Macro Variable Values

The SYMBOLGEN option is the most useful SAS option to enable as you start writing programs that contain macro variables. When SYMBOLGEN is enabled, the results of the resolution of macro variables are displayed in the SAS log. SYMBOLGEN displays the value of a macro variable in the SAS log just before the statement with the macro variable reference.

SYMBOLGEN shows the values of both automatic and user-defined macro variables.

The SYMBOLGEN option helps you debug your programs. If you are getting unexpected results when using macro variables, enable this option and read the SAS log.

It is easier to enable SYMBOLGEN than to write %PUT statements. However, SYMBOLGEN displays the values of *all* macro variables you reference in your program while %PUT lets you selectively display macro variable values. The %PUT statement gives you control of where and when a macro variable value is displayed. SYMBOLGEN only displays macro variable values when they are referenced. Macro variable values are not displayed at the time they are created with %LET.

The following program references three macro variables: two user-defined and one automatic. The OPTIONS statement enables SYMBOLGEN. (To turn off SYMBOLGEN, enter: `options nosymbolgen;`)

```
options symbolgen;

%let reptitle=Book Section;
%let reptvar=section;

title "Frequencies by &reptitle as of &sysday";
proc freq data=books.ytdsales;
   tables &reptvar;
run;

title "Means by &reptitle as of &sysday";
proc means data=books.ytdsales;
   class &reptvar;
   var salepric;
run;
```

The SAS log looks like this:

```
16    options symbolgen;
17
18    %let reptitle=Book Section;
19    %let reptvar=section;
20
SYMBOLGEN:  Macro variable REPTITLE resolves to Book Section
SYMBOLGEN:  Macro variable SYSDAY resolves to Saturday
21    title "Frequencies by &reptitle as of &sysday";
22    proc freq data=books.ytdsales;
SYMBOLGEN:  Macro variable REPTVAR resolves to section
23       tables &reptvar;
24    run;

NOTE: The PROCEDURE FREQ used 1.54 seconds.

SYMBOLGEN:  Macro variable REPTITLE resolves to Book Section
SYMBOLGEN:  Macro variable SYSDAY resolves to Saturday
25    title "Means by &reptitle as of &sysday";
26    proc means data=books.ytdsales;
SYMBOLGEN:  Macro variable REPTVAR resolves to section
27       class &reptvar;
28       var salepric;
29    run;

NOTE: The PROCEDURE MEANS used 0.5 seconds.
```

Understanding Automatic Macro Variables

When a SAS session is invoked, a set of macro variables are automatically defined by the SAS System. The macro processor maintains these variables and their values in the macro symbol table. You can use these macro variables anywhere in your SAS programs other than in data lines. Typically automatic macro variables are used to store information about your SAS session such as time of day the SAS session was invoked, version of SAS, and site number.

Several automatic macro variables are listed in Table 3.1. A more complete list is in Appendix A.

There are three types of automatic macro variables. The macro variables in Table 3.1 are grouped by type.

The first type of automatic macro variable has values fixed at the start of the SAS session; these values never change during the SAS session. The values of the second type are also set at the start of the SAS session, but these values can be changed by the SAS System. The values of the third type are initialized at the start of the SAS session and can be modified by you or the SAS System.

Table 3.1   A sample of automatic macro variables

Type of automatic macro variable	Automatic Macro Variable	Description
Values remain fixed	SYSDATE	the character value that is equal to the date the SAS session started in DATE7. format
	SYSDATE9	the character value that is equal to the date the SAS session started in DATE9. format. (Version 7)
	SYSDAY	text of the day of the week the SAS session started
	SYSVER	the character value representing the release number of SAS software that is executing
	SYSTIME	the character value representing the time the SAS session started
Values can be changed by the SAS System	SYSERR	return code set at end of each DATA step and most PROC steps
	SYSLIBRC	return code from most recent LIBNAME statement
Values can be changed by you or by the SAS System	SYSDSN	name of the most recently created data set in two fields: WORK TEMP
	SYSLAST	name of the most recently created data set in one field: WORK.TEMP

The values of all automatic macro variables are text values —even the date and time values are treated as text.

The SYS prefix is reserved for automatic macro variables. Avoid using this prefix when creating your own macro variables. Also, don't define any of your own macro variables with the name of an automatic macro variable. If you do, you will probably get an error message since most automatic macro variables are read-only and fixed in value at the time of their definition. The few automatic macro variables that can be modified are defined for items that can change throughout your SAS session, like last data set accessed.

Example: Using Automatic Variables

Five automatic macro variables are referenced in the following program. The automatic macro variable names are highlighted.

```
data web;
   set books.ytdsales;
   if section='Web Design' and datesold > "&sysdate"d-6;
run;

proc print data=web;
title "Web Design Titles Sold in the Past Week";
title2 "Report Date: &sysday &sysdate &systime";
footnote1 "Data Set Used: &syslast  SAS Version: &sysver";
   var title datesold salepric;
run;
```

Partial output for the above program is shown in Figure 3.2.

Figure 3.2   Partial output for program containing automatic macro variables

```
               Web Design Titles Sold in the Past Week
                  Report Date: Friday 19JUN98 14:44

      OBS       TITLE                          DATESOLD       SALEPRIC

       1        Wonderful Web Pages            06/14/98         $27.99
       2        HTML and Web Page Design       06/14/98         $24.34
       3        Creating Great Web Pages       06/15/98         $25.99
       4        Web Pages for Your Intranet    06/15/98         $25.30
       5        HTML Reference                 06/15/98         $34.99
                     .
                     .
                     .

            Data Set Used: BOOKS.YTDSALES     SAS Version: 6.12
```

Understanding User-defined Macro Variables

The applications of user-defined macro variables are limitless. User-defined macro variables can be created and referenced anywhere in your programs other than in data lines. The macro processor maintains the values of user-defined macro variables in the macro symbol table. Some of the tasks that you can accomplish with user-defined macro variables are the following:

- annotate reports

- select subsets of data sets

- pass information between SCL and the DATA step

- use as variables in macro programs.

Creating Macro Variables with the %LET Statement

One way to create and update a macro variable is with a %LET statement. The %LET statement tells the macro processor to add the macro variable to the macro symbol table if the macro variable does not exist. It also tells the macro processor to associate a text value with that macro variable name.

The %LET statement is written as follows and is terminated with a semicolon. No quotation marks are required to enclosed the macro variable value.

```
%let macro-variable-name=macro-variable-value;
```

The %LET statement can be submitted from the Program Editor window or from a SAS program. It is a SAS macro language statement, not a SAS language statement. It creates macro variables, not SAS data set variables.

The %LET statement is executed as soon as the macro processor receives it from the word scanner. For example, if you place a %LET statement within a DATA step, the %LET statement is processed before the DATA step is executed. This happens in the midst of the tokenization of the SAS language statements in the DATA step, before compilation and execution of the DATA step. The DATA step eventually executes after all the SAS language statements in the DATA step are collected by the compiler.

Examples of Using the %LET Statement

The following statements are examples of %LET statements assigning values to macro variables. Try submitting these %LET statements and also create some of your own using your own data.

```
%let nocalc=53*21 + 100.1;

%let value1=982;
%let value2=813;
%let result=&value1 + &value2;

%let reptext=This report is for ***  Department XYZ  ***;

%let region=Region 3;
```

```
%let text=Sales Report;
%let moretext="Sales Report";
%let reptitle=&text &region;
%let reptitl2=&moretext &region;

%let sentence=        This one started with leading blanks.;

%let chars=Symbols: !@#$%^&*;

%let novalue=;

%let holdvars=varnames;
%let &holdvars=title author datesold;
```

Following is the SAS log that results from submission of the above statements. A %PUT statement was added after each %LET statement to display the value of the macro variable created with the %LET statement. Text was added to the %PUT statement for the macro variable SENTENCE to more clearly show that the leading blanks were removed.

```
1      %let nocalc=53*21 + 100.1;
2      %put &nocalc;
53*21 + 100.1

3      %let value1=982;
4      %put &value1;
982
5      %let value2=813;
6      %put &value2;
813
7      %let result=&value1 + &value2;
8      %put &result;
982 + 813

9      %let reptext=This report is for ***  Department XYZ   ***;
10     %put &reptext;
This report is for ***  Department XYZ   ***

11     %let region=Region 3;
12     %put &region;
Region 3
13     %let text=Sales Report;
14     %put &text;
Sales Report
15     %let moretext="Sales Report";
16     %put &moretext;
"Sales Report"
17     %let reptitle=&text &region;
18     %put &reptitle;
Sales Report Region 3
19     %let reptitl2=&moretext &region;
20     %put &reptitl2;
"Sales Report" Region 3
```

```
21    %let sentence=        This one started with leading blanks.;
22    %put Now no leading blanks:&sentence;
Now no leading blanks:This one started with leading blanks.

23    %let chars=Symbols: !@#$%^&*;
24    %put &chars;
Symbols: !@#$%^&*

25    %let novalue=;
26    %put &novalue;


27    %let holdvars=varnames;
28    %put &holdvars;
varnames
29    %let &holdvars=title author datesold;
30    %put &holdvars;
varnames
31    %put &varnames;
title author datesold
```

Observations to make from the %LET assignments above include:

- The macro processor uses the semicolon to detect the end of the assignment of a value to a macro variable.

- All the values that were assigned are acceptable macro variable values.

- The SAS log shows that the SAS System treats all macro variable values as text. No arithmetic calculations are done. (SAS log line 1 and SAS log line 7)

- When assigning values to macro variables, quotation marks are not used to enclose the value. When quotation marks are used, the quotation marks become part of the text associated with the macro variables. (SAS log line 15) (The use of quotation marks in macro programming is a special topic in the macro facility and is discussed in Chapter 6.)

- Leading blanks are removed from the value of a macro variable. (SAS log line 21)

- Blanks and special characters are valid macro variable values. The macro processor does not interpret the & and % symbols as macro triggers when they are not followed by a letter or underscore. (SAS log line 23)

- A macro variable can have a null value. (SAS log line 25)

- You can assign macro variable values to other macro variables and combine macro variables in a %LET statement to create a new macro variable. The macro processor recognizes the & and % symbols as macro triggers when they are followed by a letter or underscore. (SAS log line 27)

Combining Macro Variables with Text

This section describes some of the interesting ways you can program with macro variables. When you combine macro variable references with text or with other macro variable references, you can create new macro variable references. These new macro variable references are resolved before the SAS language statements in which they are placed are tokenized.

A concatenation operator is not needed to combine macro variables with text. However, periods (.) act as delimiters of macro variable references and may be needed to delimit a macro variable reference that precedes text.

Placing Text Before a Macro Variable Reference

The examples that follow illustrate how you can create a new macro variable reference by placing text or other macro variable references before a macro variable reference. The underlined text indicates where macro variable references are combined with other macro variable references and text. Note that no concatenation operator was used to combine the macro variable references with text.

```
%let mosold=4;
%let level=25;

data book&mosold&level;
   set books.ytdsales(where=(month(datesold)=&mosold));

   attrib over&level length=$3 label="Cost > $&level";

   if cost > &level then over&level='YES';
   else over&level='NO';
run;

proc freq data=book&mosold&level;
title "Frequency Count of Books Sold During Month &mosold";
title2 "Grouped by Cost Over $&level";
   tables over&level;
run;
```

After the macro processor creates the two macro variables and resolves the macro variable references, the program becomes:

```
data book425;
   set books.ytdsales(where=(month(datesold)=4));

   attrib over25 length=$3 label="Cost > $25";

   if cost > 25 then over25='YES';
   else over25='NO';
```

```
run;

proc freq data=book425;
title "Frequency Count of Books Sold During Month 4";
title2 "Grouped by Cost Over $25";
  tables over25;
run;
```

With this technique, you can write a program once and reuse it for a different subset by changing the values of the macro variables. For example, changing the values of the two macro variables in the above program will produce the same report, but on different groups in the data set. Now the two %LET statements are:

```
%let mosold=12;
%let level=50;
```

After the macro processor creates the two macro variables and resolves the macro variable references, the program becomes:

```
data book1250;
  set books.ytdsales(where=(month(datesold)=12));

  attrib over50 length=$3 label="Cost > $50";

  if cost > 50 then over50='YES';
  else over50='NO';
run;

proc freq data=book1250;
title "Frequency Count of Books Sold During Month 12";
title2 "Grouped by Cost Over $50";
  tables over50;
run;
```

Placing Text After a Macro Variable Reference

When text follows a macro variable reference, a period must be placed at the end of the macro variable reference to terminate it. The macro processor recognizes that a period signals the end of a macro variable name and determines that the name of the macro variable is the text between the ampersand and the period. All macro variable references can be terminated with periods.

The examples in the preceding section do not require terminating periods for proper resolution of the macro variable references. A space or semicolon after the macro variable reference delimits the macro variable reference. The macro processor knows that blanks and semicolons cannot be part of a macro variable name. When a macro variable reference is placed after another macro variable reference, the ampersand of the second macro variable reference delimits the previous macro variable reference.

In the following example, text follows macro variable references. No periods follow the macro variable references. The goal of the PROC step is to compute frequency counts for the responses to the first five questions of a customer survey: QUES1, QUES2, QUES3, QUES4, and QUES5. However, this program cannot be tokenized and it does not execute.

```
*----WARNING: This program does not execute;
%let prefix=QUES;

proc freq data=books.survey;
   var &prefix1 &prefix2 &prefix3 &prefix4 &prefix5;
run;
```

After resolving the macro variable references, the program becomes:

```
proc freq data=books.survey;
   var &prefix1 &prefix2 &prefix3 &prefix4 &prefix5;
run;
```

The following messages are listed in the SAS log.

```
WARNING: Apparent symbolic reference PREFIX1 not resolved.
WARNING: Apparent symbolic reference PREFIX2 not resolved.
WARNING: Apparent symbolic reference PREFIX3 not resolved.
WARNING: Apparent symbolic reference PREFIX4 not resolved.
WARNING: Apparent symbolic reference PREFIX5 not resolved.
```

The five macro variables PREFIX1, PREFIX2, PREFIX3, PREFIX4, and PREFIX5 have not been defined in the program. Therefore, the macro processor cannot resolve the five macro variable references. The macro processor sends the macro variable references back to the input stack as they were received. The word scanner cannot tokenize the VAR statement. The PROC FREQ step does not execute.

Delimiters are added to the program below to tell the macro processor when the macro variable references end. Now the macro variable references resolve as desired, and the text that follows the references is concatenated to the results of the resolution. The corrected code looks like this:

```
*----This program executes correctly;
%let prefix=QUES;

proc freq data=books.survey;
   var &prefix.1 &prefix.2 &prefix.3 &prefix.4 &prefix.5;
run;
```

The macro processor substitutes QUES for the &PREFIX macro variable reference. After macro variable resolution, the program becomes:

```
proc freq data=books.survey;
  var QUES1 QUES2 QUES3 QUES4 QUES5;
run;
```

Concatenating Permanent SAS Data Set Names and Catalog Names with Macro Variables

The macro processor understands that periods delimit macro variable references. Periods are also used in the SAS language to refer to permanent data sets and catalogs. Permanent data sets and catalogs have multi-part names, each part delimited with a period.

When macro variable references are concatenated with permanent data set names or catalog names, your coding must distinguish the role of the period in your statement. Does the period terminate the macro variable reference or is it part of the name of a data set or catalog?

When a macro variable reference precedes the period in a data set or catalog name, add one extra period after the macro variable reference. The macro processor looks up the macro variable reference delimited by the first period. It determines the macro variable name is complete because of the terminating period. The macro variable value is put on the input stack and the word scanner tokenizes it. The word scanner recognizes the second period as text. That second period is then part of the data set name or catalog name.

The following program illustrates the necessity of using two periods.

```
*----WARNING: This program does not execute;
%let survlib=BOOKSURV;

proc freq data=&survlib.survey1;
  tables age;
run;
```

After macro variable resolution, the program becomes:

```
*----WARNING: This program does not execute;
proc freq data=BOOKSURVsurvey1;
  tables age;
run;
```

The macro processor does its work before the PROC FREQ statement is completely tokenized. In this example, the word scanner suspends processing when it encounters the macro variable reference. The macro processor looks up the &SURVLIB macro variable. This reference is terminated with a period. The macro processor interprets that period as terminating the macro variable reference. The macro processor finds the value for &SURVLIB which is BOOKSURV and puts BOOKSURV on top of the input stack. The rest of the data set name, SURVEY1, now ends up being concatenated to BOOKSURV. The period could only be used once and the macro processor used it first. The program cannot execute because the data set BOOKSURVSURVEY1 does not exist.

To make the program correctly resolve the macro variable reference and access the permanent data set BOOKSURV.SURVEY1, add another period. The macro processor is done with its work after seeing the first period. The rest of the data set name, .SURVEY1, is now concatenated to BOOKSURV.

```
*----This program executes;
%let survlib=BOOKSURV;

proc freq data=&survlib..survey1;
  tables age;
run;
```

After macro variable resolution, the program becomes:

```
*----This program executes;
proc freq data=BOOKSURV.survey1;
  tables age;
run;
```

Referencing Macro Variables Indirectly

When working with a series of macro variables, a technique called indirect referencing adds more flexibility to your macro programming. In an indirect macro variable reference, the resolution of a macro variable reference leads to the resolution of another macro variable reference.

The macro variable references that have been described so far are written with one ampersand preceding the macro variable name. This is a direct reference to a macro variable. For some applications, it has been necessary to add a period to delimit the macro variable reference.

In indirect referencing, more than one ampersand precedes a macro variable reference. The macro processor follows specific rules in resolving references with multiple ampersands. You can take advantage of these rules to create new macro variable references.

The rules that the macro processor uses to resolve macro variable references that contain multiple ampersands follow.

- Macro variable references are resolved from left to right.

- Two ampersands (&&) resolve to one ampersand (&).

- Multiple leading ampersands cause the macro processor to rescan the reference until no more ampersands can be resolved.

Resolving Two Ampersands that Precede a Macro Variable Reference

The first example of indirectly referencing macro variables follows. Five macro variables define five sections in the computer department of the bookstore. A report program analyzes sales information for a section. The macro variable N represents the section number. In the following example, the sales information is produced for section 3, Operating Systems.

The indirect macro variable reference in this program is &&SECTION&N. Note that there are two ampersands preceding SECTION. The macro processor scans the macro variable reference twice, once for each of the preceding ampersands.

```
%let section1=Internet;
%let section2=Networking and Communication;
%let section3=Operating Systems;
%let section4=Programming Languages;
%let section5=Web Design;

*----Look for section number defined by macro var n;
%let n=3;
proc means data=books.ytdsales;
   title "Sales for Section: &&section&n";
   where section="&&section&n";
   var salepric;
run;
```

After macro variable resolution, the above program becomes:

```
proc means data=books.ytdsales;
   title "Sales for Section: Operating Systems";
   where section="Operating Systems";
   var salepric;
run;
```

What happens if only one ampersand precedes SECTION? The reference would be &SECTION&N.

The macro processor resolves &SECTION&N in two parts: &SECTION and &N. &N can be resolved. In the example, &N equals 3. The macro variable &SECTION is not defined and cannot be resolved. A warning message is written to the SAS log window. The following statements demonstrate how &SECTION&N does not resolve as desired.

```
options symbolgen;
%let section3=Operating Systems;
%let n=3;

%put &section&n;
```

The SAS log of the above code is as follows.

```
1      options symbolgen;
2      %let section3=Operating Systems;
3      %let n=3;
4
5      %put &section&n;
WARNING: Apparent symbolic reference SECTION not resolved.
```

The process of resolving the macro variable references is shown in Figure 3.3.

Figure 3.3   How two concatenated macro variable references are resolved

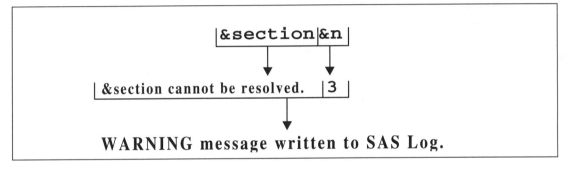

To resolve the macro variable reference as desired, add another ampersand before SECTION: &&SECTION&N. This forces the macro processor to scan the reference twice.

On the first pass, the two ampersands are resolved to one and the reference to &N is resolved to 3 yielding &SECTION3. On the second pass, the macro variable reference &SECTION3 is resolved to Operating Systems. This is shown in Figure 3.4.

Chapter 3: Macro Variables **63**

Figure 3.4   Using two ampersands to force the macro processor to scan a macro variable reference twice

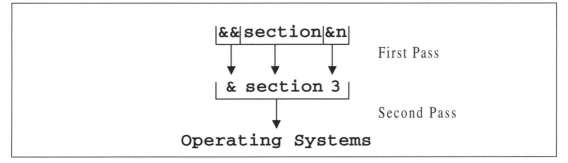

The above code is modified to include another ampersand before SECTION.

```
options symbolgen;
%let section3=Operating Systems;
%let n=3;

%put &&section&n;
```

The SAS log follows.

```
6     options symbolgen;
7     %let section3=Operating Systems;
8     %let n=3;
9
10    %put &&section&n;
SYMBOLGEN:  && resolves to &.
SYMBOLGEN:  Macro variable N resolves to 3
SYMBOLGEN:  Macro variable SECTION3 resolves to Operating
Systems
Operating Systems
```

The SYMBOLGEN option traces the resolution of indirect macro variable references. With SYMBOLGEN enabled, the SAS log of the first program in this section follows.

```
132   options symbolgen;
133   %let section1=Programming Languages;
134   %let section2=Web Design;
135   %let section3=Operating Systems;
136   %let section4=Networking;
137   %let section5=Internet;
138   *----Look for section number defined by macro var n;
139   %let n=3;
140   proc means data=books.ytdsales;
SYMBOLGEN:  && resolves to &.
SYMBOLGEN:  Macro variable N resolves to 3
```

```
SYMBOLGEN:  Macro variable SECTION3 resolves to Operating
Systems
141    title "Sales for Section: &&section&n";
142    where section="&&section&n";
SYMBOLGEN:  && resolves to &.
SYMBOLGEN:  Macro variable N resolves to 3
SYMBOLGEN:  Macro variable SECTION3 resolves to Operating
Systems
143    var salepric;
144  run;

NOTE: The PROCEDURE MEANS used 0.11 seconds.
```

Resolving Multiple Ampersands before a Macro Variable Reference

The next example illustrates how the macro processor resolves multiple ampersands preceding a macro variable reference. Three ampersands precede the macro variable reference.

This program provides flexibility in specifying the WHERE statement for a PROC MEANS step. The macro variable, WHEREVAR, is assigned the name of the data set variable that defines the WHERE selection. In the example, the goal is to compute PROC MEANS for section 3, Operating Systems.

```
options symbolgen;
%let section1=Internet;
%let section2=Networking and Communication;
%let section3=Operating Systems;
%let section4=Programming Languages;
%let section5=Web Design;
%let dept1=Computer;
%let dept2=Reference;
%let dept3=Science;

%let n=3;
%let wherevar=section;

proc means data=books.ytdsales;
   title "Sales for &wherevar: &&&wherevar&n";
   where &wherevar="&&&wherevar&n";
   var salepric;
run;
```

The SAS log for this program follows. Note how SYMBOLGEN traces each scanning step in the resolution of the macro variable reference.

```
30    options symbolgen;
31    %let section1=Internet;
32    %let section2=Networking and Communication;
33    %let section3=Operating Systems;
```

```
34     %let section4=Programming Languages;
35     %let section5=Web Design;
36     %let dept1=Computer;
37     %let dept2=Reference;
38     %let dept3=Science;
39
40     %let n=3;
41     %let wherevar=Section;
42
43     proc means data=books.ytdsales;
SYMBOLGEN:  Macro variable WHEREVAR resolves to Section
SYMBOLGEN:  && resolves to &.
SYMBOLGEN:  Macro variable WHEREVAR resolves to Section
SYMBOLGEN:  Macro variable N resolves to 3
SYMBOLGEN:  Macro variable SECTION3 resolves to Operating
Systems
44        title "Sales for &wherevar: &&&wherevar&n";
SYMBOLGEN:  Macro variable WHEREVAR resolves to Section
45        where &wherevar="&&&wherevar&n";
SYMBOLGEN:  && resolves to &.
SYMBOLGEN:  Macro variable WHEREVAR resolves to Section
SYMBOLGEN:  Macro variable N resolves to 3
SYMBOLGEN:  Macro variable SECTION3 resolves to Operating
Systems
46        var salepric;
47     run;

NOTE: The PROCEDURE MEANS used 1.04 seconds.
```

The macro processor scans the reference &&&WHEREVAR&N twice. Figure 3.5 shows how the macro processor breaks down this reference.

Figure 3.5   How the macro processor resolves a multiple ampersand macro variable reference

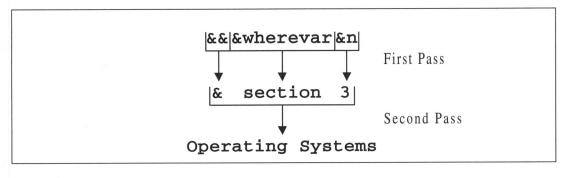

CHAPTER 4

Macro Programs

A macro program is another tool for text substitution. Macro programs are like macro variables: text is associated with a name. The difference is that the text that is substituted by a macro program can be created using macro language programming statements. These macro language statements allow you to write more complicated instructions for the macro processor than what you can write with macro variables alone.

Each macro program is assigned a name. When the macro program is referenced in your SAS program, the statements inside the macro program execute. The text that results from the execution is substituted into your SAS program at the location of the macro program reference.

Macro programs use macro variables and macro language statements to generate the text that builds your SAS programs. The SAS macro programming language has the same type of statements as other programming languages. Many macro language statements resemble their SAS language counterparts.

Several macro language statements can only be used inside macro programs. The macro language statements that we have seen so far, %LET and %PUT, can be used inside or outside macro programs. Macro language statements and macro variable references placed outside a macro program, like we've seen in the last chapter, are referred to as being in open code.

This chapter describes how to create and use macro programs.

Creating Macro Programs

A macro program is defined with the following statements:

```
%MACRO program;
    <text>
%MEND program;
```

where:

%MACRO marks the beginning of the macro program definition.

program is the name assigned to the macro program. The macro program name must be a valid SAS name; that is, it must be no more than 8 characters in length under Version 6, no more than 32 characters in Version 7, and must start with a letter or underscore with the remaining characters any combination of letters, numbers, and underscores.

The macro program name must not be a reserved word in the macro facility (see Appendix B). Note that the macro program name is not preceded with a percent sign on the %MACRO statement.

<text> is any combination of

- text strings

- macro variables, macro functions, or macro language statements

- SAS programming statements. SAS programming statements are treated as text within the macro program definition.

%MEND marks the end of the macro program. Including the macro program name on the %MEND statement is optional.

The options that can be included on the %MACRO statement are described later.

An example of a macro program follows.

```
%macro sales;
   title "Sales Report for Week Ending &sysdate";
   proc gchart data=temp;
     where today()-6 <= datesold <= today();
     hbar section / sumvar=profit type=sum;
   run;
%mend sales;
```

To compile this macro program for use later in your SAS session, submit the macro program definition from the Program Editor or from within your SAS program. The word scanner tokenizes the macro program and sends the tokens to the macro processor for compilation.

When the macro processor compiles the macro language statements in the macro program, it saves the results in a SAS catalog. By default, macro programs are stored in a catalog in the WORK library. The name of the catalog is SASMACR. Macro programs can also be saved in permanent catalogs. This is described in Chapter 8.

A compiled macro program can be reused within the same SAS session. A macro program only has to be submitted once in your SAS session. The compiled macro program remains in the SASMACR catalog throughout the SAS session. When the SAS session ends, the SASMACR catalog containing the compiled macro program is deleted by the SAS System.

After submitting the program above from the Program Editor, the WORK directory looks like Figure 4.1. Currently, one catalog, the SASMACR catalog, exists.

Figure 4.1   The results of the DIR command

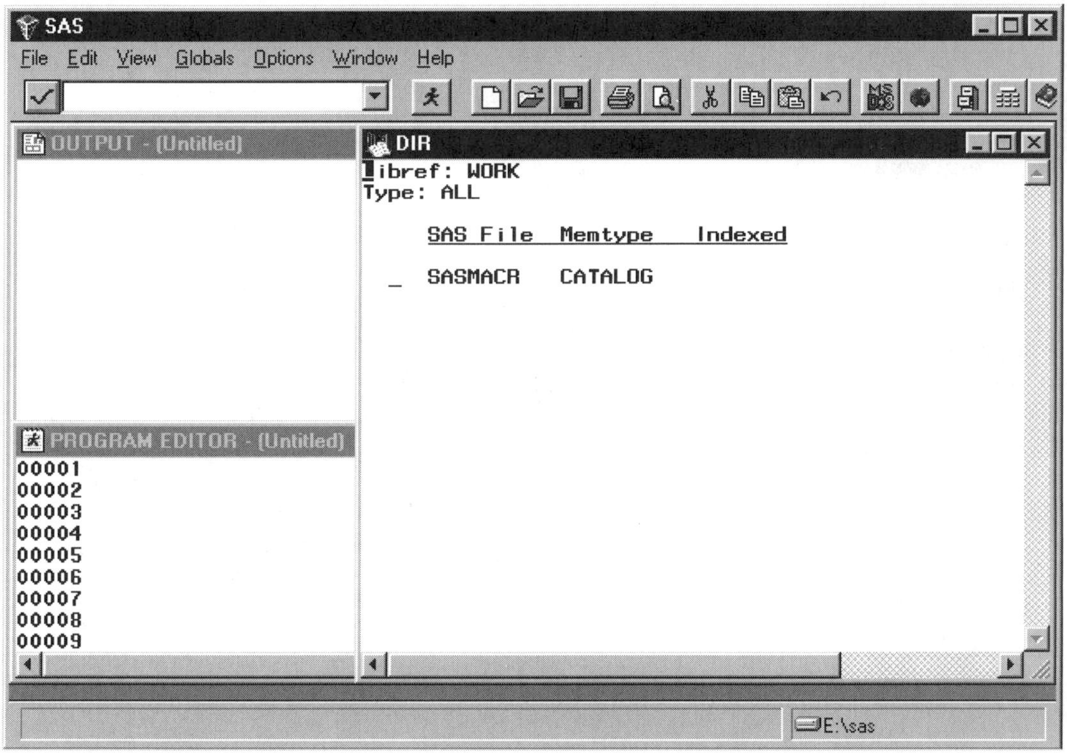

When you view the contents of the SASMACR catalog, the following window in Figure 4.2 is displayed. Note that the SALES macro program is in this catalog. The entry in the catalog for SALES is the compiled version of SALES. The compiled version cannot be viewed.

Figure 4.2   Contents of the WORK.SASMACR catalog

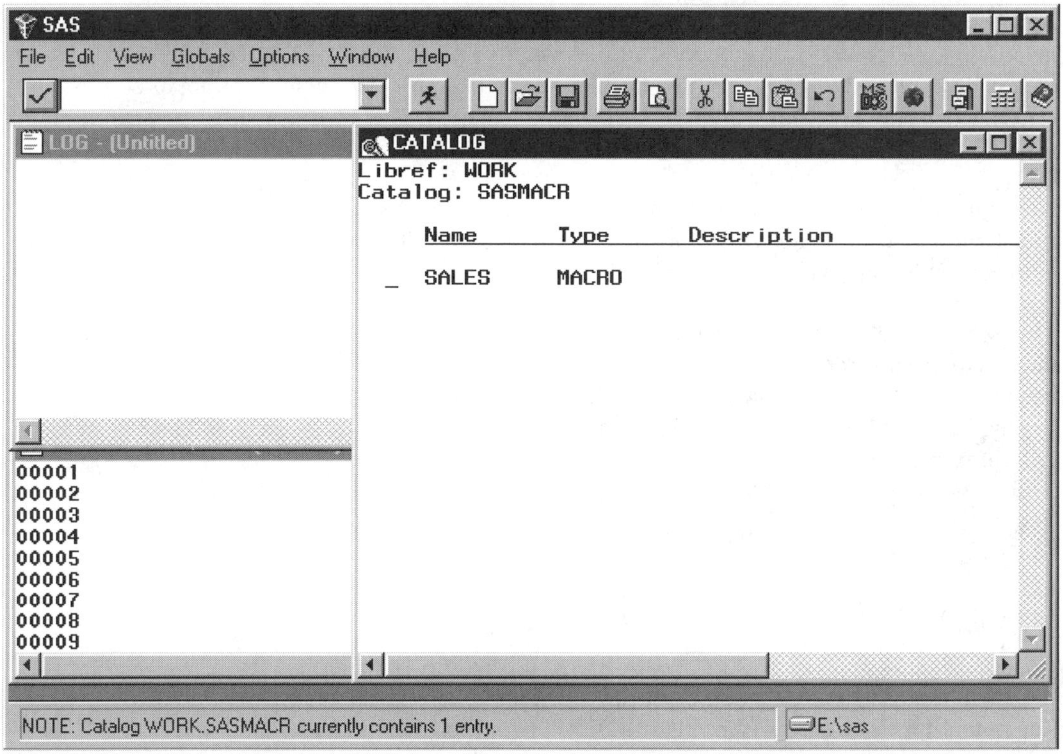

```
SAS                                                              _ □ ×
File  Edit  View  Globals  Options  Window  Help
✓                        ▼    𝄪  □ 🖙 🖫  🖨 🖺  🖿 🗐 🗐 ↶  🖾 ● 🖨 🖳 ◆
┌─ LOG - (Untitled)            ┌─ CATALOG                        _ □ ×
│                              │ Libref: WORK
│                              │ Catalog: SASMACR
│                              │
│                              │    Name       Type      Description
│                              │
│                              │  _ SALES      MACRO
│
│
│
│
│ ◀
│ 00001
│ 00002
│ 00003
│ 00004
│ 00005
│ 00006
│ 00007
│ 00008
│ 00009
│ ◀                           ◀                                   ▶
└────────────────────────────────────────────────────────────────
 NOTE: Catalog WORK.SASMACR currently contains 1 entry.      🖵 E:\sas
```

You can also list the entries in WORK.SASMACR catalog by submitting the following PROC CATALOG step.

```
proc catalog c=work.sasmacr;
   contents;
run;
quit;
```

Executing a Macro Program

A macro program is executed by submitting a reference to the macro program. To execute a macro program, submit the following statement from the Program Editor or from within your SAS program.

```
%program
```

where *program* is the name assigned to the macro program.

A reference to a macro program that has been successfully compiled may be placed anywhere in your SAS program except in data lines. This call to the macro program is preceded by a percent sign(%). The percent sign tells the word scanner to direct processing to the macro processor. The macro processor takes over and looks for the compiled program in the WORK.SASMACR catalog of session compiled macro programs. If found, the macro processor completes any processing steps needed and directs execution of the compiled macro program. If not found, an error message is written to the SAS log.

No semicolon follows the call to the macro program. The call to a macro program is not a SAS statement. Indeed, using a semicolon to terminate the call to the macro program may cause errors in the execution of your macro program.

The following SAS program, hereafter referred to as the Book Sales program, contains a call to the macro program defined in the previous section. Assume that the macro program has already been submitted so its compiled code is in the macro catalog. The program was submitted on Friday, June 12, 1998. When the SAS program is submitted, the DATA step and the SAS macro program are executed.

```
data temp;
   set books.ytdsales;
   attrib profit label='Sale Price-Cost' format=dollar8.2;
   profit=salepric-cost;
run;

%sales
```

The output for the program is in Figure 4.3.

Figure 4.3   Output for sample program containing a call to a macro program

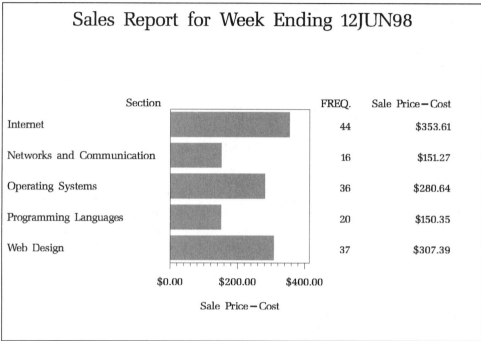

Displaying Messages in the SAS Log about Macro Program Processing

The SAS options MPRINT and MLOGIC write information about the processing of macro programs to the SAS log. These options assist you in debugging and reviewing your macro programs. The SYMBOLGEN option described earlier displays information about macro variables. SYMBOLGEN displays information about macro variables that are created in open code or inside macro programs.

Following is the SAS log of the Book Sales program, where MPRINT and MLOGIC are not enabled. The last NOTE and the WARNING are all the information we have about the SAS language statements submitted for processing by the macro program SALES.

```
517   options nosymbolgen nomprint nomlogic;
518   data temp;
519      set books.ytdsales;
520      attrib profit label='Sale Price-Cost' format=dollar8.2;
521      profit=salepric-cost;
522   run;
```

```
NOTE: The data set WORK.TEMP has 6959 observations and 11
variables.
NOTE: The DATA statement used 1.42 seconds.

523
524  %sales
```

**WARNING: The value of SECTION will be truncated to 16
characters.**
NOTE: The PROCEDURE CHART used 0.33 seconds.

Using MPRINT to Display the SAS Statements Submitted by a Macro Program

Normally when you submit a SAS program, processing messages about the compilation and execution of the SAS language statements are written to the SAS log. By default, processing messages about SAS language statements submitted from within a macro program are not written to the SAS log. If you want to see these processing messages, enable the MPRINT option.

The SAS log that follows is for the Book Sales program when the MPRINT option is enabled. Now you can verify the SAS language statements that have been submitted by the macro program.

```
525  options nosymbolgen mprint nomlogic;
526  data temp;
527     set books.ytdsales;
528     attrib profit label='Sale Price-Cost' format=dollar8.2;
529     profit=salepric-cost;
530  run;

NOTE: The data set WORK.TEMP has 6959 observations and 12
variables.
NOTE: The DATA statement used 1.42 seconds.

531
532  %sales
MPRINT(SALES):    TITLE "Sales Report for Week Ending 12JUN98";
MPRINT(SALES):    PROC GCHART DATA=TEMP;
MPRINT(SALES):    WHERE TODAY()-6 <= DATESOLD <= TODAY();
MPRINT(SALES):    HBAR SECTION / SUMVAR=PROFIT TYPE=SUM;
MPRINT(SALES):    RUN;

WARNING: The values of SECTION have been truncated to 16
characters.
NOTE: The PROCEDURE CHART used 4.45 seconds.
```

Using the MLOGIC Option to Trace Execution of a Macro Program

The MLOGIC option traces the execution of macro programs. The information written to the SAS log when MLOGIC is enabled includes the beginning and ending of the macro program and the results of arithmetic and logical macro language operations. The MLOGIC option is useful for debugging macro language statements in macro programs. The SAS log of the Book Sales program with MLOGIC enabled follows. Examples in Chapter 6 that deal with macro programming statements further illustrate the usefulness of this option.

```
573  options nosymbolgen nomprint mlogic;
574  data temp;
575     set books.ytdsales;
576     attrib profit label='Sale Price-Cost' format=dollar8.2;
577     profit=salepric-cost;
578  run;

NOTE: The data set WORK.TEMP has 6959 observations and 12
variables.
NOTE: The DATA statement used 1.42 seconds.

MLOGIC(SALES):  Beginning execution.
579
580  %sales

WARNING: The value of SECTION will be truncated to 16
characters.
NOTE: The PROCEDURE CHART used 0.39 seconds.

MLOGIC(SALES):  Ending execution.
```

Passing Values to a Macro Program through Macro Parameters

Macro program parameters expand the reusability and flexibility of your macro programs by allowing you to initialize macro variables inside your macro programs. When you use parameters, macro program code does not have to be modified each time you want the macro variables to start out with different values. Think of macro programs with parameters as similar to subroutines in other programming languages.

Macro parameter names are specified on the %MACRO statement. The names assigned to the parameters must be the same as the names of the macro variables that you want to initialize inside the macro program.

The initial values of the parameters are specified on the call to the macro program. When the macro program starts, the corresponding macro variables are initialized with the values of the parameters.

The two types of macro program parameters, positional and keyword, are described in the next two sections.

Specifying Positional Parameters in Macro Programs

Positional macro program parameters define a one-to-one correspondence between the list of parameters on the %MACRO statement and the values of the parameters on the macro program call. The general format of a macro program definition containing positional parameters is

```
%macro program(positional-1, positional-2, ...,positional-n);

    macro program referencing the macro variables in the
    positional parameter list

%mend program;
```

Positional parameters are enclosed in parentheses and are separated with commas. There is no limit to the number of positional parameters that can be defined. However, too many positional parameters can make it unwieldy to write the call to the macro program.

When you call a macro program that uses positional parameters, you must specify the same number of values in the macro program call as the number of parameters listed on the %MACRO statement. Valid values include null values and text. To specify a null value, use a comma as a placeholder.

The general format of a call to a macro program that uses positional parameters is

```
%program(value-1, value-2, ..., value-n)
```

Example: Defining a Macro Program with Positional Parameters

The next SAS program defines a macro program that uses three positional parameters and calls that macro program twice.

```
options mprint mlogic;

%macro listparm(start,stop,opts);
   title "Books Sold by Section Between &start and &stop";
   proc means data=books.ytdsales &opts;
     where "&start"d le datesold le "&stop"d;
     class section;
     var salepric;
   run;
%mend listparm;

*----First call to LISTPARM, all 3 parameters specified;
%listparm(01JUN1998,15JUN1998,n sum)
```

```
*----Second call to LISTPARM, first 2 parameters specifed and;
*----third parameter is null;
%listparm(01SEP1998,15SEP1998,)
```

The first call to LISTPARM specifies values for each of the three parameters. The three parameters are separated by commas. The third parameter specifies two options, N and SUM, for the PROC MEANS step.

A null value is specified for the third parameter in the second call to the macro program. The parameters are separated by commas. Nothing follows the second comma, so no options are added to the PROC MEANS statement. The default options on PROC MEANS are used.

Note how the SAS statements are resolved differently for each call to LISTPARM. Also note how the MLOGIC option displays the parameter values at the start of macro program execution.

The SAS log for the first call to LISTPARM follows.

```
224  *----First call to LISTPARM, all 3 parameters specified;
225  %listparm(01JUN1998,15JUN1998,n sum)
MLOGIC(LISTPARM):  Beginning execution.
MLOGIC(LISTPARM):  Parameter START has value 01JUN1998
MLOGIC(LISTPARM):  Parameter STOP has value 15JUN1998
MLOGIC(LISTPARM):  Parameter OPTS has value n sum
MPRINT(LISTPARM):   TITLE "Books Sold by Section Between
01JUN1998 and 15JUN1998";
MPRINT(LISTPARM):   PROC MEANS DATA=BOOKS.YTDSALES N SUM;
MPRINT(LISTPARM):   WHERE "01JUN1998"D LE DATESOLD LE
"15JUN1998"d;
MPRINT(LISTPARM):   CLASS SECTION;
MPRINT(LISTPARM):   VAR SALEPRIC;
MPRINT(LISTPARM):   RUN;

NOTE: The PROCEDURE MEANS used 0.28 seconds.

MLOGIC(LISTPARM):  Ending execution.
```

The SAS log for the second call to LISTPARM follows.

```
MLOGIC(LISTPARM):  Beginning execution.
MLOGIC(LISTPARM):  Parameter START has value 01SEP1998
MLOGIC(LISTPARM):  Parameter STOP has value 15SEP1998
MLOGIC(LISTPARM):  Parameter OPTS has value
226  *----Second call to LISTPARM, first 2 parameters specifed;
227  *----third parameter is null;
228  %listparm(01SEP1998,15SEP1998,)
MPRINT(LISTPARM):   TITLE "Books Sold by Section Between
01SEP1998 and 15SEP1998";
MPRINT(LISTPARM):   PROC MEANS DATA=BOOKS.YTDSALES ;
MPRINT(LISTPARM):   WHERE "01SEP1998"D LE DATESOLD LE
"15SEP1998"d;
```

```
MPRINT(LISTPARM):    CLASS SECTION;
MPRINT(LISTPARM):    VAR SALEPRIC;
MPRINT(LISTPARM):    RUN;

NOTE: The PROCEDURE MEANS used 0.28 seconds.

MLOGIC(LISTPARM):    Ending execution.
```

Specifying Keyword Parameters in Macro Programs

A macro program with many parameters is easier to define and use with keyword parameters rather than positional parameters. With keyword parameters, you do not have to keep track of the positions of the parameters when writing the call to the macro program.

A call to a macro program that has been defined with keyword parameters contains both the parameter names and the initial parameter values. On the %MACRO statement defining the macro program, an equal sign (=) follows each parameter name.

Another advantage of using keyword parameters is that you can specify default values for the keyword parameters when the macro program is defined. Then, when you want to use a default value, you can omit the keyword parameter completely from the macro program call.

Keyword parameters can be specified in any order. A one-to-one correspondence between the parameters on the %MACRO statement and the values on the call to the macro program is not required. The general format of a macro program definition containing keyword macro program parameters is

```
%macro program(keyword1=value, keyword2=value, ...,
keywordn=value);

    macro program referencing the macro variables in the keyword
    parameter list

%mend program;
```

Keyword parameter lists are enclosed in parentheses and keyword references are separated with commas. In the previous code, *keyword1, keyword2,* and so on represent the names of the parameters and the corresponding macro variables in the macro program.

The values following the equal signs are the default values passed to the macro program. It is not necessary to specify default values for keyword parameters. However, if a default value has been defined and you want to call the macro program and use that default value, you do not have to specify the corresponding keyword parameter in the macro program call.

There is no limit to the number of keyword parameters that can be defined.

The general format of a call to a macro program that uses keyword parameters is:

```
%program(keyword1=value1,keyword2=value2,...,keywordn=valuen)
```

Valid keyword parameter values include null values and text. In a macro program call, no value after the equal sign of a parameter initializes the macro variable with a null value.

Example: Defining a Macro Program with Keyword Parameters

The next SAS program defines a macro program and calls that macro program three times. The macro program uses keyword parameters. The second call to the macro program specifies a null value for a keyword parameter value. The third call to the macro program shows how default values are used. The SAS log for each of the three calls to KEYPARM follows the macro program definition.

```
options mprint mlogic;

%macro keyparm(start=01JAN1998,stop=31DEC1998,
               opts=N SUM MIN MAX);
   title "Books Sold by Section Between &start and &stop";
   proc means data=books.ytdsales &opts;
     where "&start"d le datesold le "&stop"d;
     class section;
     var salepric;
   run;
%mend keyparm;

*----First call to KEYPARM: specify all keyword parameters;
%keyparm(start=01JUN1998,stop=15JUN1998,opts=n sum)

*----Second call to KEYPARM: specify start and stop,;
*----opts is null: should see default stats for PROC MEANS;
%keyparm(start=01SEP1998,stop=15SEP1998,opts=)

*----Third call to KEYPARM: use defaults for start and stop,;
*----specify opts;
%keyparm(opts=n sum)
```

All three parameters are specified in the first call to the KEYPARM macro program. The SAS log for the first call to KEYPARM follows.

```
299  *---- First call to KEYPARM: specify all keyword
parameters;
300  %keyparm(start=01JUN1998,stop=15JUN1998,opts=n sum)
MLOGIC(KEYPARM):  Beginning execution.
MLOGIC(KEYPARM):  Parameter START has value 01JUN1998
MLOGIC(KEYPARM):  Parameter STOP has value 15JUN1998
MLOGIC(KEYPARM):  Parameter OPTS has value n sum
MPRINT(KEYPARM):   TITLE "Books Sold by Section Between
```

```
01JUN1998 and 15JUN1998";
MPRINT(KEYPARM):    PROC MEANS DATA=BOOKS.YTDSALES N SUM;
MPRINT(KEYPARM):    WHERE "01JUN1998"D LE DATESOLD LE
"15JUN1998"d;
MPRINT(KEYPARM):    CLASS SECTION;
MPRINT(KEYPARM):    VAR SALEPRIC;
MPRINT(KEYPARM):    RUN;

NOTE: The PROCEDURE MEANS used 0.27 seconds.

MLOGIC(KEYPARM):    Ending execution.
```

In the second call to KEYPARM, a null value is specified for the OPTS parameter. That means that the null value replaces the default value. The result is that the statistics keywords —N, SUM, MIN, and MAX —are not on the PROC MEANS statement. Instead, the default statistics for PROC MEANS are calculated. The SAS log for the second call to KEYPARM follows.

```
MLOGIC(KEYPARM):    Beginning execution.
MLOGIC(KEYPARM):    Parameter START has value 01SEP1998
MLOGIC(KEYPARM):    Parameter STOP has value 15SEP1998
MLOGIC(KEYPARM):    Parameter OPTS has value
301
302   *----Second call to KEYPARM: specify start and stop,;
303   *----opts is null: should see default stats for PROC
MEANS;
304   %keyparm(start=01SEP1998,stop=15SEP1998,opts=)
MPRINT(KEYPARM):    TITLE "Books Sold by Section Between
01SEP1998 and 15SEP1998";
MPRINT(KEYPARM):    PROC MEANS DATA=BOOKS.YTDSALES ;
MPRINT(KEYPARM):    WHERE "01SEP1998"D LE DATESOLD LE
"15SEP1998"d;
MPRINT(KEYPARM):    CLASS SECTION;
MPRINT(KEYPARM):    VAR SALEPRIC;
MPRINT(KEYPARM):    RUN;

NOTE: The PROCEDURE MEANS used 0.27 seconds.

MLOGIC(KEYPARM):    Ending execution.
```

Only the OPTS parameter is specified on the third call. The START and STOP keywords are omitted. Therefore, PROC MEANS computes the N and SUM statistics on observations that fall between the default dates specified for START and STOP: January 1, 1998 and December 31, 1998. The SAS log for the third call to KEY PARM follows.

```
MLOGIC(KEYPARM):    Beginning execution.
MLOGIC(KEYPARM):    Parameter OPTS has value n sum
MLOGIC(KEYPARM):    Parameter START has value 01JAN1998
MLOGIC(KEYPARM):    Parameter STOP has value 31DEC1998
305
```

```
306  *----Third call to KEYPARM: use defaults for start and 307
stop,; *----specify opts;
308  %keyparm(opts=n sum)
```
MPRINT(KEYPARM):   TITLE "Books Sold by Section Between
01JAN1998 and **31DEC1998**";
MPRINT(KEYPARM):   PROC MEANS DATA=BOOKS.YTDSALES **N SUM**;
MPRINT(KEYPARM):   WHERE "**01JAN1998**"D LE DATESOLD LE
"**31DEC1998**"d;
MPRINT(KEYPARM):   CLASS SECTION;
MPRINT(KEYPARM):   VAR SALEPRIC;
MPRINT(KEYPARM):   RUN;

NOTE: The PROCEDURE MEANS used 0.55 seconds.

MLOGIC(KEYPARM):   Ending execution.

Specifying Mixed Parameter Lists in Macro Programs

Positional parameters and keyword parameters can both be defined for the same macro program.
Positional parameters must be placed ahead of keyword parameters. Otherwise, the same rules for
defining and using each type of parameter apply.

The general format of a macro program definition containing positional parameters and keyword
parameters is

```
%macro program(positional-1, positional-2, ...,positional-n,
    keyword1=value,keyword2=value, ...,  keywordm=value);

  macro program referencing both kinds of parameters

%mend program;
```

The general format of a call to a macro program that contains positional parameters and keyword
parameters is

```
%program(positionalvalue-1, positionalvalue-2, ...,
    positionalvalue-n,
    keyword1=value, keyword2=value, ...,  keywordm=value)
```

Example: Defining a Macro Program with Positional Parameters and Keyword Parameters

The following SAS program defines a macro program with positional parameters and keyword
parameters and calls that macro program. The macro program MIXDPARM calls PROC MEANS.
The two positional parameters, STATS and OTHROPTS, allow selection of PROC MEANS

options. The two keyword parameters, START and STOP, specify a date range for the calculations.

On the call to MIXDPARM, a null value is specified for the STATS positional parameter; the default PROC MEANS statistics are calculated. OTHROPTS is initialized with the value MISSING. The STOP keyword parameter is not specified. Therefore, the default value of December 31, 1998 is used as the stop date.

```
options mprint mlogic;

%macro mixdparm(stats,othropts,start=01JAN1998,stop=31DEC1998);
   title "Books Sold by Section Between &start and &stop";
   proc means data=books.ytdsales &stats &othropts;
     where "&start"d le datesold le "&stop"d;
     class section;
     var salepric;
   run;
%mend mixdparm;

%mixdparm(,missing,start=01DEC1998)
```

The SAS log for the call to MIXDPARM follows.

```
343   %mixdparm(,missing,start=01DEC1998)
MLOGIC(MIXDPARM):  Beginning execution.
MLOGIC(MIXDPARM):  Parameter STATS has value
MLOGIC(MIXDPARM):  Parameter OTHROPTS has value missing
MLOGIC(MIXDPARM):  Parameter START has value 01DEC1998
MLOGIC(MIXDPARM):  Parameter STOP has value 31DEC1998
MPRINT(MIXDPARM):    TITLE "Books Sold by Section Between
01DEC1998 and 31DEC1998";
MPRINT(MIXDPARM):    PROC MEANS DATA=BOOKS.YTDSALES MISSING;
MPRINT(MIXDPARM):    WHERE "01DEC1998"D LE DATESOLD LE
"31DEC1998"D;
MPRINT(MIXDPARM):    CLASS SECTION;
MPRINT(MIXDPARM):    VAR SALEPRIC;
MPRINT(MIXDPARM):    RUN;

NOTE: The PROCEDURE MEANS used 0.33 seconds.

MLOGIC(MIXDPARM):  Ending execution.
```

CHAPTER 5

More on Mechanics of Macro Processing

As your macro programming applications become more complex, an understanding of the technical aspects of macro processing becomes more important. This knowledge will likely speed up development and debugging of your programs.

The discussion of the technical aspects of macro processing that began in Chapter 2 is continued in this chapter. Symbol tables, both global and those created for macro programs, are described. The processing of a macro program is illustrated.

Understanding Macro Symbol Tables

There are two types of macro symbol tables: global and local. The global macro symbol table, as the name implies, stores macro variables that can be referenced throughout your SAS session, both from open code and from within macro programs. A local macro symbol table stores macro variables defined within a macro program. References to these macro variables can only be resolved locally, from within the macro program that defined them.

At the start of a SAS session, the macro processor creates the global macro symbol table to store the values of automatic macro variables. The global macro symbol table also stores the values of the macro variables that you create in open code.

A local macro symbol table is created by executing a macro program that contains macro variables. The macro variables that are defined in the macro program are stored in the local macro symbol table associated with the macro program. These local macro variables by default can only be referenced from within the macro program. A local macro symbol table is deleted when the macro program that is associated with it ends.

As your SAS programming assistant, the macro processor keeps track of the domain of each macro variable that is defined in your SAS program. The context in which you reference a macro variable directs the macro processor's search for the macro variable value.

Figure 5.1 presents an example of how the domains of the macro symbol tables are defined by default. Two macro programs, M1 and M2, are invoked. In addition, two more macro programs, M2A and M2B, are invoked from within macro program M2 when macro program M2 is executing.

Observations to make from Figure 5.1 include:

- Macro variables in the global macro symbol table may be referenced in open code and from within M1, M2, M2A, and M2B.

- The macro variables that are created by M1 are only available to M1.

- The macro variables that are created by M2 can be referenced by M2A and M2B.

- The macro variables that are created by M2A are only available to M2A.

- The macro variables that are created by M2B are only available to M2B.

Figure 5.1　Example of macro symbol tables in a SAS session

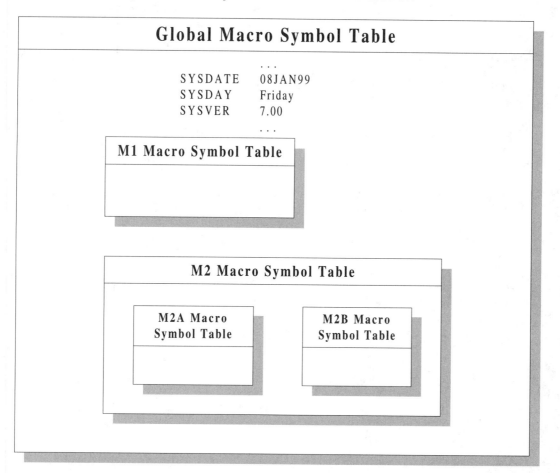

Understanding the Global Macro Symbol Table

The macro processor creates the global macro symbol table at the start of a SAS session. The first macro variables that are placed in the global macro symbol table are the automatic macro variables that the SAS System defines. For example, the automatic macro variables, SYSDATE, SYSDAY, and SYSVER, are stored in the global macro symbol table.

User-defined macro variables may also be added to the global macro symbol table. The user-defined macro variables created in Chapter 3 were all stored in the global macro symbol table. There are three ways that you can add macro variables to the global macro symbol table:

- Create the macro variable in open code.

- List the macro variable on a %GLOBAL statement in the macro program in which it is defined.

- Create the macro variable in a DATA step with the SAS language routine CALL SYMPUT. (The CALL SYMPUT routine provides an interface between the SAS DATA step and the macro processor, and it is described in Chapter 7.)

Global macro variables can be referenced throughout the SAS session in which they are created. They may be referenced from open code and from inside macro programs. You can modify the values of user-defined global macro variables throughout your SAS session. As described in Chapter 3, you may modify a few of the automatic macro variables as well.

The following program creates a macro variable in open code and references it both from open code and from within a macro program. The domain of the macro variable is the global macro symbol table because it was created in open code. Therefore, the macro variable can be successfully referenced and resolved both from open code and from within a macro program.

```
options symbolgen mprint;

%let subset=Internet;

%macro makeds;
   data temp;
      set books.ytdsales(where=(section="&subset"));
      attrib mosold label='Month of Sale';
      mosold=month(datesold);
   run;
%mend makeds;

%makeds

proc tabulate data=temp;
title "Book Sales as of &sysdate";
   class mosold;
   var salepric listpric;
   tables mosold all,
          (salepric listpric)*(n*f=6. sum*f=dollar12.2) /
          box="Section: &subset";
   keylabel all='** Total **';
run;
```

When the program is executed, the SAS log looks like this:

```
135   options symbolgen mprint;
136
137   %let subset=Internet;
138
139   %macro makeds;
140     data temp;
141       set books.ytdsales(where=(section="&subset"));
142       attrib mosold label='Month of Sale';
143       mosold=month(datesold);
144     run;
145   %mend makeds;
146
147   %makeds
MPRINT(MAKEDS):    DATA TEMP;
SYMBOLGEN:  Macro variable SUBSET resolves to Internet
MPRINT(MAKEDS):    SET
BOOKS.YTDSALES(WHERE=(SECTION="Internet"));
MPRINT(MAKEDS):    ATTRIB MOSOLD LABEL='Month of Sale';
MPRINT(MAKEDS):    MOSOLD=MONTH(DATESOLD);
MPRINT(MAKEDS):    RUN;

NOTE: The data set WORK.TEMP has 322 observations and 11
      variables.
NOTE: The DATA statement used 0.66 seconds.


148
149   proc tabulate data=temp;
SYMBOLGEN:  Macro variable SYSDATE resolves to 25MAR98
150   title "Book Sales as of &sysdate";
151     class mosold;
152     var salepric listpric;
153     tables mosold all,
154           (salepric listpric)*(n*f=6. sum*f=dollar12.2) /
155           box="Section: &subset";
SYMBOLGEN:  Macro variable SUBSET resolves to Internet
156     keylabel all='** Total **';
157   run;

NOTE: The PROCEDURE TABULATE used 0.33 seconds.
```

The output for this program is shown in Figure 5.2.

Figure 5.2   Output for macro program MAKEDS using global macro variable SUBSET

```
                       Book Sales as of 25MAR98                        1

   ----------------------------------------------------------------
   |Section:          |    Sale Price      |     List Price        |
   |Internet          |-------------------+-------------------|
   |                  |   N   |    SUM     |   N   |    SUM        |
   |-------------+------+-----------+------+-----------|
   |Month of Sale |      |           |      |           |
   |-------------|      |           |      |           |
   |1            |   105|  $3,246.67|   105|  $3,320.75|
   |-------------+------+-----------+------+-----------|
   |2            |   120|  $3,725.94|   120|  $3,812.00|
   |-------------+------+-----------+------+-----------|
   |3            |    97|  $2,848.16|    97|  $2,911.15|
   |-------------+------+-----------+------+-----------|
   |** Total **  |   322|  $9,820.78|   322| $10,043.90|
   ----------------------------------------------------------------
```

A representation of the global macro symbol table that results when the macro program executes is in Figure 5.3. Since no macro variables are created by the MAKEDS macro program, no local macro symbol table for MAKEDS is created.

Figure 5.3   The global macro symbol table when MAKEDS executes

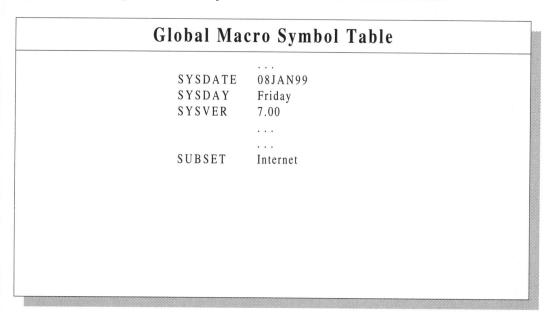

Global Macro Symbol Table

	. . .
SYSDATE	08JAN99
SYSDAY	Friday
SYSVER	7.00
	. . .
	. . .
SUBSET	Internet

Understanding Local Macro Symbol Tables

If your macro program creates macro variables, the macro processor creates a local macro symbol table whenever that macro program executes. A local macro symbol table stores the values of the macro variables that are created by the macro program. When the macro program finishes, the macro processor deletes the associated local macro symbol table.

It is important to understand the boundaries of the macro symbol tables. By default, the domain of macro variables that are created in a macro program is local to the macro program that defines them. For a given local macro variable, if no identically named macro variable is defined as global, a reference that is made in open code to that macro variable cannot be resolved.

A macro program may also be called from within another macro program. The macro program that is invoked from within another macro program may reference the macro variables created by the macro program that invoked it. Looking back at Figure 5.1, the macro programs M2A and M2B are called by macro program M2. The local macro variables that are created by M2 are available to M2A and M2B. Conversely, the macro program M2 cannot resolve references to local macro variables created by M2A or M2B.

Therefore, you can have multiple macro variables, each with the same name, in one SAS session. Obviously, this can become confusing and is something to avoid, at least while you are learning how to write macro programs.

Macro parameters are always local to the macro program that defines them. These macro variables are stored in the local macro symbol table associated with the macro program. You cannot make these macro variables global, but you can assign their values to global macro variables.

The program in the previous section is revised below so that a parameter passes to MAKEDS the value that defines the subset. Now the macro variable SUBSET is stored in the local macro symbol table that is associated with the MAKEDS macro program. SUBSET is stored in the MAKEDS macro symbol table because it is defined as a parameter to MAKEDS. The macro variable SUBSET is not available globally.

```
options symbolgen mprint;

%macro makeds(subset);
  data temp;
    set books.ytdsales(where=(section="&subset"));
    attrib mosold label='Month of Sale';
    mosold=month(datesold);
  run;
%mend makeds;

%makeds(Internet)

proc tabulate data=temp;
title "Book Sales as of &sysdate";
  class mosold;
  var salepric listpric;
  tables mosold all,
         (salepric listpric)*(n*f=6. sum*f=dollar12.2) /
         box="Section: &subset";
  keylabel all='** Total **';
run;
```

The SAS log for the revised program follows.

```
23   options symbolgen mprint;
24
25   %macro makeds(subset);
26     data temp;
27       set books.ytdsales(where=(section="&subset"));
28       attrib mosold label='Month of Sale';
29       mosold=month(datesold);
30     run;
31   %mend makeds;
32
33   %makeds(Internet)
MPRINT(MAKEDS):   DATA TEMP;
SYMBOLGEN:  Macro variable SUBSET resolves to Internet
MPRINT(MAKEDS):   SET
BOOKS.YTDSALES(WHERE=(SECTION="Internet"));
MPRINT(MAKEDS):   ATTRIB MOSOLD LABEL='Month of Sale';
```

```
MPRINT(MAKEDS):    MOSOLD=MONTH(DATESOLD);
MPRINT(MAKEDS):    RUN;

NOTE: The data set WORK.TEMP has 322 observations and 11
variables.
NOTE: The DATA statement used 0.77 seconds.

34
35    proc tabulate data=temp;
SYMBOLGEN:   Macro variable SYSDATE resolves to 25MAR98
36    title "Book Sales";
37       class mosold;
38       var salepric listpric;
39       tables mosold all,
40             (salepric listpric)*(n*f=6. sum*f=dollar12.2) /
41             box="Section: &subset";
WARNING: Apparent symbolic reference SUBSET not resolved.
42       keylabel all='** Total **';
43    run;

NOTE: The PROCEDURE TABULATE used 0.39 seconds.
```

Note the warning in the PROC TABULATE step that the macro variable reference to SUBSET could not be resolved. The reference to the macro variable SUBSET in the PROC TABULATE step is in open code, outside of the MAKEDS macro program. By the time PROC TABULATE executes, the MAKEDS macro program has ended and the MAKEDS symbol table has already been deleted. At that point, the macro processor only searches the global macro symbol table to resolve the SUBSET macro variable reference.

The output for this program is shown in Figure 5.4.

Figure 5.4   Output for macro program MAKEDS using local macro variable SUBSET

```
┌─────────────────────────────────────────────────────────────────┐
│                  Book Sales as of 25MAR98                    1    │
│                                                                   │
│   ------------------------------------------------------------    │
│   |Section:        |     Sale Price      |     List Price     |   │
│   |&subset         |--------------------+--------------------|   │
│   |                |   N  |    SUM       |   N  |    SUM      |   │
│   |------------+------+------------+------+------------|   │
│   |Month of Sale |      |            |      |            |   │
│   |------------|      |            |      |            |   │
│   |1              |  105|   $3,246.67|  105|   $3,320.75|   │
│   |------------+------+------------+------+------------|   │
│   |2              |  120|   $3,725.94|  120|   $3,812.00|   │
│   |------------+------+------------+------+------------|   │
│   |3              |   97|   $2,848.16|   97|   $2,911.15|   │
│   |------------+------+------------+------+------------|   │
│   |** Total  **   |  322|   $9,820.78|  322|  $10,043.90|   │
│   ------------------------------------------------------------    │
└─────────────────────────────────────────────────────────────────┘
```

Figure 5.5 provides a representation of the global macro symbol table and the local macro symbol table when the macro program executes.

Figure 5.5   The macro symbol tables during execution of the MAKEDS macro program when SUBSET is a local macro variable

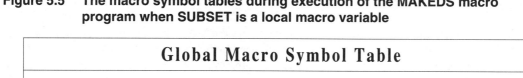

Global Macro Symbol Table
. . .

SYSDATE	08JAN99
SYSDAY	Friday
SYSVER	7.00

. . .

MAKEDS Macro Symbol Table
SUBSET   Internet

Here are two ways to revise the program so that the reference to SUBSET in the PROC TABULATE step can be resolved. The easier of the two is shown first. This program places the PROC TABULATE step within the MAKEDS macro program.

```
options symbolgen mprint;

%macro makeds(subset);
  data temp;
    set books.ytdsales(where=(section="&subset"));
    attrib mosold label='Month of Sale';
    mosold=month(datesold);
  run;

  proc tabulate data=temp;
  title "Book Sales as of &sysdate";
    class mosold;
    var salepric listpric;
    tables mosold all,
          (salepric listpric)*(n*f=6. sum*f=dollar12.2) /
          box="Section: &subset";
    keylabel all='** Total **';
  run;
%mend makeds;

%makeds(Internet)
```

In the second version, the %GLOBAL statement instructs the macro processor to create a macro variable and store it in the global macro symbol table. Then the value of the SUBSET macro variable is assigned to this global macro variable within the MAKEDS macro program. Now the value of a local macro variable can be transferred to a global macro variable. The macro variable reference in PROC TABULATE is changed to the name of the global macro variable, GLSUBSET.

```
options symbolgen mprint;

%macro makeds(subset);
  %global glsubset;
  %let glsubset=&subset;

  data temp;
    set books.ytdsales(where=(section="&subset"));
    attrib mosold label='Month of Sale';
    mosold=month(datesold);
  run;
%mend makeds;

%makeds(Internet)

proc tabulate data=temp;
title "Book Sales as of &sysdate";
  class mosold;
  var salepric listpric;
  tables mosold all,
         (salepric listpric)*(n*f=6. sum*f=dollar12.2) /
         box="Section: &glsubset";
  keylabel all='** Total **';
run;
```

The SAS log for this second version follows.

```
230   options symbolgen mprint;
231
232   %macro makeds(subset);
233      %global glsubset;
234      %let glsubset=&subset;
235
236      data temp;
237         set books.ytdsales(where=(section="&subset"));
238         attrib mosold label='Month of Sale';
239         mosold=month(datesold);
240      run;
241   %mend makeds;
242
243   %makeds(Internet)
SYMBOLGEN:  Macro variable SUBSET resolves to Internet
MPRINT(MAKEDS):    DATA TEMP;
SYMBOLGEN:  Macro variable SUBSET resolves to Internet
```

```
MPRINT(MAKEDS):    SET
BOOKS.YTDSALES(WHERE=(SECTION="Internet"));
MPRINT(MAKEDS):    ATTRIB MOSOLD LABEL='Month of Sale';
MPRINT(MAKEDS):    MOSOLD=MONTH(DATESOLD);
MPRINT(MAKEDS):    RUN;

NOTE: The data set WORK.TEMP has 322 observations and 11
      variables.
NOTE: The DATA statement used 0.66 seconds.


244
245  proc tabulate data=temp;
SYMBOLGEN:  Macro variable SYSDATE resolves to 25MAR98
246  title "Book Sales as of &sysdate";
247     class mosold;
248     var salepric listpric;
249     tables mosold all,
250           (salepric listpric)*(n*f=6. sum*f=dollar12.2) /
251           box="Section: &glsubset";
SYMBOLGEN:  Macro variable GLSUBSET resolves to Internet
252     keylabel all='** Total **';
253  run;

NOTE: The PROCEDURE TABULATE used 0.33 seconds.
```

Figure 5.6 provides a representation of the macro symbol tables after the %LET statement inside the MAKEDS macro program executes.

Figure 5.6   The macro symbol tables after %LET inside MAKEDS has executed

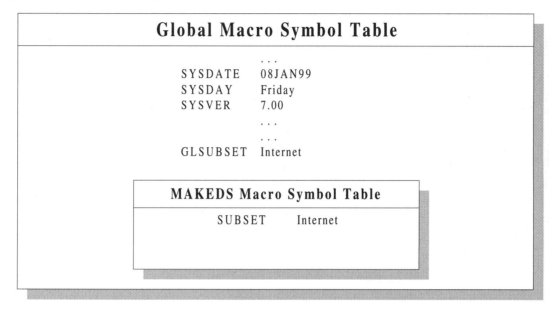

Working with Global Macro Variables and Local Macro Variables

The macro processor follows a specific set of rules to resolve macro variable references. The context in which you place a macro variable reference tells the macro processor which symbol table to begin with in its search for the macro variable.

When you ask the macro processor to resolve a macro variable reference, the macro processor first looks in the most local domain of that macro variable. If the macro variable is called from within a macro program, the most local domain of the macro variable is the local macro symbol table associated with the macro program. If the macro variable is not in the most local domain, the macro processor moves to the next higher domain. The search stops when the macro processor reaches the domain of the global macro symbol table. If the macro variable cannot be found in the global macro symbol table, an error message is issued.

When a global macro variable is referenced within a macro program, the macro processor does not by default create a local macro variable with that name. Instead, the macro processor uses the global macro variable.

When you define more than one macro program in your SAS program, the order of the macro program definitions does not matter. Further, if one macro program calls another, you do not have to nest the definition of the called macro program within the definition of the first. Each macro program definition is its own entity, like a subroutine. Indeed, it will probably be easier to read your code if you do not nest macro program definitions.

The macro processor follows the path in Figure 5.7 when it is creating or modifying macro variables.

Figure 5.7   How the macro processor accesses symbol tables when it creates or modifies macro variables

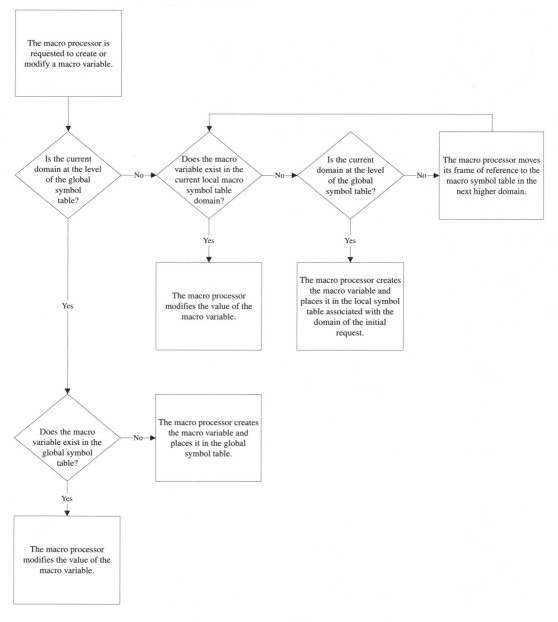

The process that the macro processor follows when it resolves a macro variable reference is shown in Figure 5.8.

Figure 5.8   How the macro processor accesses symbol tables when it resolves a macro variable reference

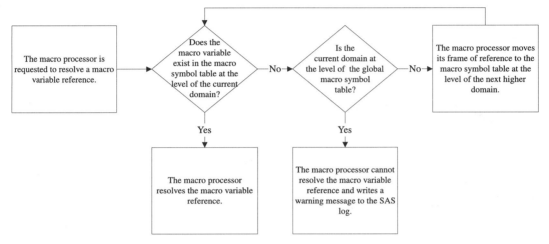

Defining the Domain of a Macro Variable by Using the %GLOBAL or %LOCAL Macro Language Statement

The %GLOBAL and %LOCAL macro language statements explicitly direct where the macro processor stores macro variables. These statements can override the rules described in the previous section as well as help document your programs.

The syntax of both statements is

```
%GLOBAL macro-variable(s) ;
%LOCAL macro-variable(s) ;
```

The %GLOBAL statement tells the macro processor to create the macro variables listed on the statement and to store them in the global macro symbol table. The macro processor initially sets these macro variables to a null value. These macro variables can be used throughout the SAS session. The %GLOBAL statement can be used in open code or inside a macro program. A %GLOBAL statement was used in the section on local macro symbol tables.

The macro processor places the macro variables listed on the %LOCAL statement in the domain of the macro program in which the %LOCAL statement was issued. The %LOCAL statement can only be used within a macro program. The macro processor will only look in the local domain to resolve references to macro variables on the %LOCAL statement.

The next program uses the same name for two different macro variables. The two macro variables have different domains.

```
options symbolgen mprint;

%global subset;
%let subset=Internet;

%macro loclmvar;
  %local subset;
  %let subset=Web Design;

  proc means data=books.ytdsales n sum maxdec=2;
  title "Book Sales as of &sysdate";
  title2 "Uses LOCAL SUBSET macro variable: &subset";
    where section="&subset";
    var salepric;
  run;
%mend loclmvar;

%loclmvar

proc means data=books.ytdsales n sum maxdec=2;
title "Book Sales as of &sysdate";
title2 "Uses GLOBAL SUBSET macro variable: &subset";
  where section="&subset";
  var salepric;
run;
```

The SAS log for the above program follows.

```
417   options symbolgen mprint;
418
419   %global subset;
420   %let subset=Internet;
421
422   %macro loclmvar;
423     %local subset;
424     %let subset=Web Design;
425
426     proc means data=books.ytdsales n sum maxdec=2;
427     title "Book Sales as of &sysdate";
428     title2 "Uses LOCAL SUBSET macro variable: &subset";
429       where section="&subset";
430       var salepric;
431     run;
432   %mend loclmvar;
433
```

```
434  %loclmvar
MPRINT(LOCLMVAR):    PROC MEANS DATA=BOOKS.YTDSALES N SUM
MAXDEC=2;
SYMBOLGEN:  Macro variable SYSDATE resolves to 29MAR98
MPRINT(LOCLMVAR):    TITLE "Book Sales as of 29MAR98";
SYMBOLGEN:  Macro variable SUBSET resolves to Web Design
MPRINT(LOCLMVAR):    TITLE2 "Uses LOCAL SUBSET macro variable:
Web Design";
SYMBOLGEN:  Macro variable SUBSET resolves to Web Design
MPRINT(LOCLMVAR):    WHERE SECTION="Web Design";
MPRINT(LOCLMVAR):    VAR SALEPRIC;
MPRINT(LOCLMVAR):    RUN;

NOTE: The PROCEDURE MEANS used 0.22 seconds.

435
436  proc means data=books.ytdsales n sum maxdec=2;
SYMBOLGEN:  Macro variable SYSDATE resolves to 29MAR98
437  title "Book Sales as of &sysdate";
SYMBOLGEN:  Macro variable SUBSET resolves to Internet
438  title2 "Uses GLOBAL SUBSET macro variable: &subset";
439    where section="&subset";
SYMBOLGEN:  Macro variable SUBSET resolves to Internet
440    var salepric;
441  run;

NOTE: The PROCEDURE MEANS used 0.27 seconds.
```

The output for this program is shown in Figure 5.9.

**Figure 5.9   Output for program with same name for a local macro variable and a
global macro variable**

```
                    Book Sales as of 25MAR98                    1
              Uses LOCAL SUBSET macro variable: Web Design

                    Analysis Variable : SALEPRIC Sale Price

                       N              Sum
                   -----------------
                      356         10797.11



                    Book Sales as of 25MAR98                    2
              Uses GLOBAL SUBSET macro variable: Internet

                    Analysis Variable : SALEPRIC Sale Price

                       N              Sum
                   -----------------
                      322          9820.78
                   -----------------
```

A representation of the macro symbol tables when the LOCLMVAR macro program executes is in
Figure 5.10.

Figure 5.10 The macro symbol tables when LOCLMVAR executes

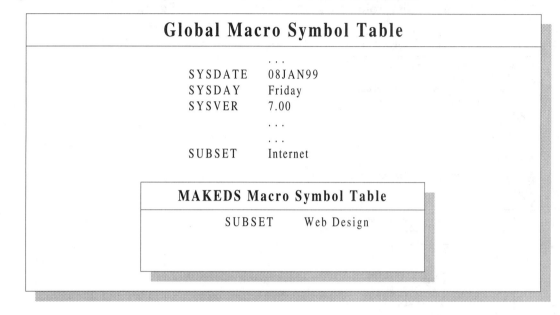

Processing of Macro Programs

Understanding how macro programs are compiled and executed will help you more quickly write and debug SAS programs that contain macro language. This section describes how macro programs are processed by the SAS System and the macro facility.

How a Macro Program Is Compiled

The SAS program in Figure 5.11 contains a macro program definition and a call to the macro program. The path that the SAS System follows in compiling the macro program definition is described in the remaining figures in this section.

Figure 5.11 A SAS program with a macro program definition and a call to the macro program has been submitted for processing

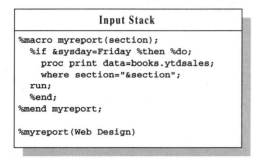

```
                    Input Stack

%macro myreport(section);
  %if &sysday=Friday %then %do;
    proc print data=books.ytdsales;
    where section="&section";
  run;
  %end;
%mend myreport;

%myreport(Web Design)
```

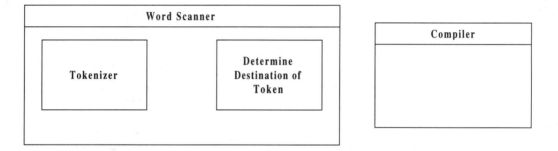

Word Scanner		Compiler
Tokenizer	Determine Destination of Token	

Macro Processor	Global Macro Symbol Table
	SAS Automatic Macro Variables
	SYSDATE 11DEC98
	SYSDAY Friday
	SYSVER 7.00
	.
	.
	.

Tokenization of the program begins in Figure 5.12.

Figure 5.12 Statements are transferred from the input stack to the word scanner

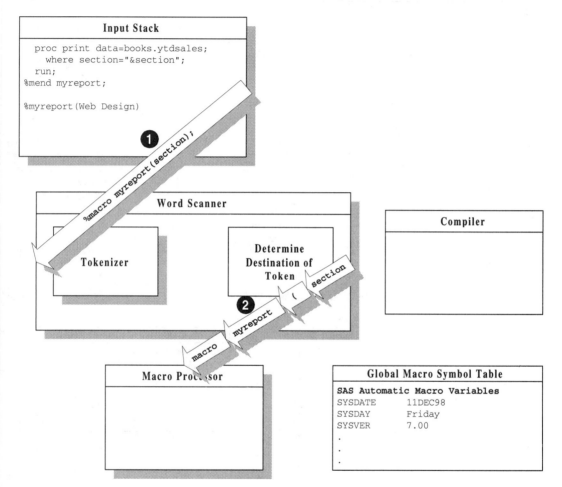

The two steps in Figure 5.12 are as follows:

❶ The MACRO statement is passed to the word scanner for tokenization

❷ The word scanner detects a percent sign followed by a nonblank character and sends subsequent tokens to the macro processor.

In Figure 5.13 the word scanner continues to send tokens to the macro processor.

Figure 5.13 Tokens continue to be transferred to the macro processor

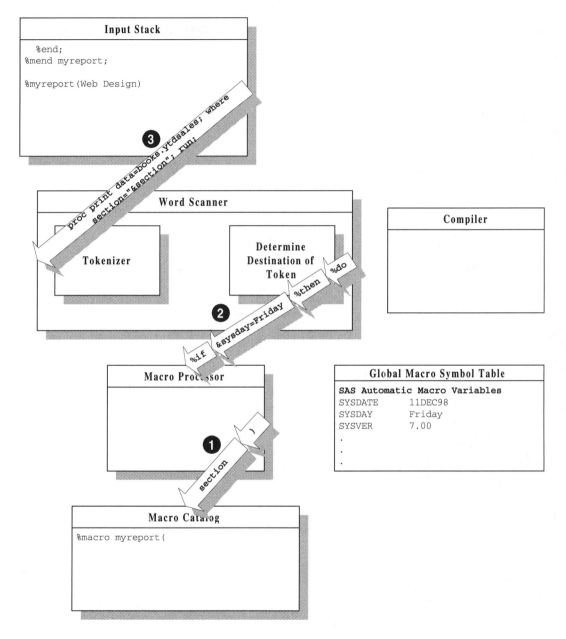

The three steps in Figure 5.13 are as follows:

1 An entry in the macro catalog for macro program MYREPORT is created.

2 The tokens from the %IF statement are passed to the macro processor. The expression &SYSDAY=Friday is considered one token.

3 The entire PROC PRINT step is considered one text token and is passed to the macro processor for storage with the MYREPORT macro program.

In Figure 5.14, compilation of the macro statements in MYREPORT is complete. The expression &SYSDAY=Friday is stored as text and will not be resolved until MYREPORT is executed. The PROC PRINT step is stored as text and will not be tokenized and compiled until MYREPORT is executed.

Figure 5.14 Compilation of macro program MYREPORT is complete

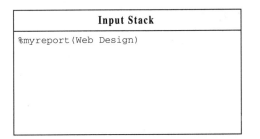

```
Input Stack
%myreport(Web Design)
```

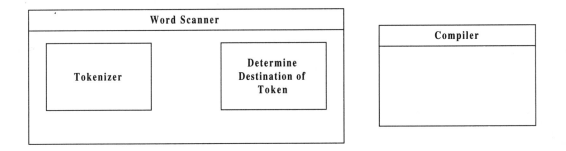

```
Word Scanner

Tokenizer          Determine
                   Destination of
                   Token
```

```
Compiler
```

```
Macro Processor
```

```
Global Macro Symbol Table

SAS Automatic Macro Variables
SYSDATE     11DEC98
SYSDAY      Friday
SYSVER      7.00
  .
  .
  .
```

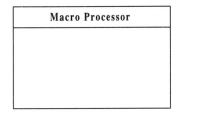

```
Macro Catalog

%macro myreport(section);
  %if &sysday=Friday %then %do;
    proc print data=books.ytdsales;
      where section="&section";
    run;
  %end;
%mend myreport;
```

How a Macro Program Is Executed

The example in the previous section is continued in this section. A call to the macro program MYREPORT is executed. This process is described in the figures in this section.

In Figure 5.15, the macro program MYREPORT has been called with a value assigned to the parameter SECTION.

Figure 5.15 The macro program MYREPORT has been called and begins executing

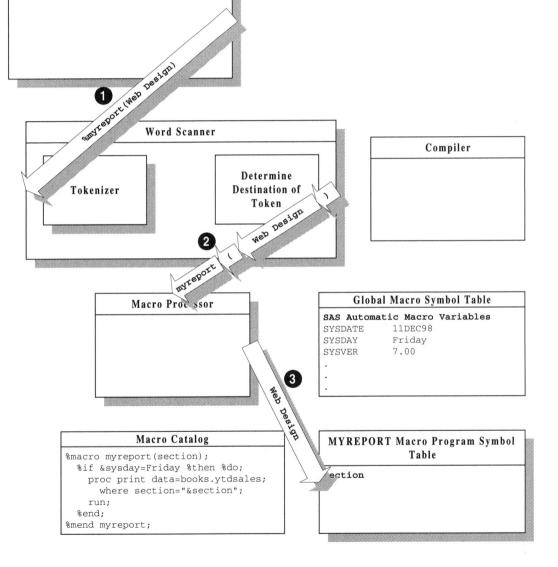

The three steps in Figure 5.15 are as follows:

❶ The macro program MYREPORT has been called.

❷ The word scanner detects the percent sign and transfers tokens to the macro processor.

❸ The macro processor begins executing macro program MYREPORT. A macro symbol table is created for the macro program. The macro variable SECTION is added to the MYREPORT symbol table. The initial value for SECTION that is passed as a parameter to the macro program MYREPORT is placed in the symbol table.

In Figure 5.16, the macro processor starts executing MYREPORT.

Figure 5.16 The macro program MYREPORT continues executing

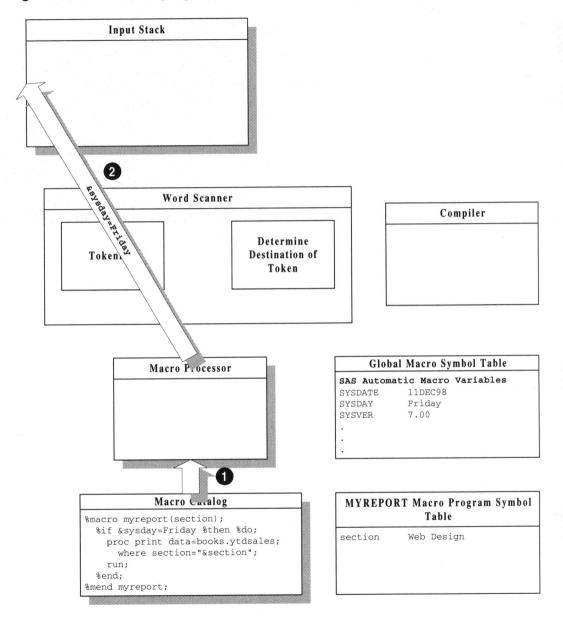

The two steps in Figure 5.16 are as follows:

❶ The macro processor executes the compiled %IF statement.

❷ The macro processor puts the text &SYSDAY=FRIDAY on the input stack so that it can be tokenized by the word scanner.

Next the word scanner tokenizes the &SYSDAY=Friday expression and directs resolution of the macro variable reference to the macro processor.

Figure 5.17 The word scanner receives the &SYSDAY=Friday expression for tokenization and evaluation of the expression is passed to the macro processor

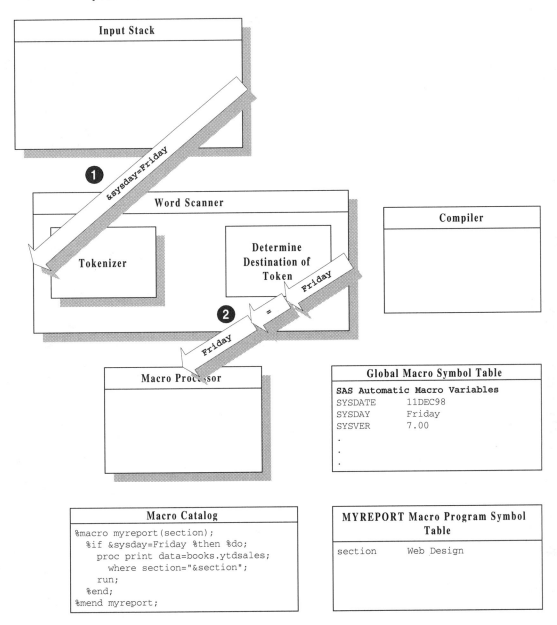

The two steps in Figure 5.17 are as follows:

❶ The word scanner receives the &SYSDAY=Friday expression.

❷ After receiving the resolved value of &SYSDAY from the macro processor, the word scanner sends the tokens to the macro processor for evaluation.

Assume that MYREPORT was run on a Friday. Therefore, the %IF condition is true. The statements in the PROC PRINT step are placed in the input stack by the macro processor. Execution of MYREPORT continues in Figure 5.18.

Figure 5.18 The PROC PRINT step is tokenized and the macro variable reference to &SECTION is resolved

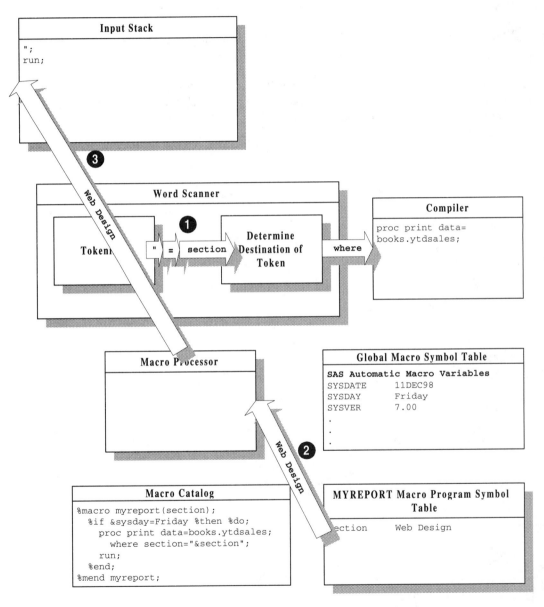

The steps in Figure 5.18 are as follows:

 The SAS language statements are tokenized by the word scanner and passed to the compiler.

❷ The reference to &SECTION is resolved. The reference to &SECTION is made within the MYREPORT macro program. The macro symbol table for MYREPORT is the first place the macro processor looks to resolve &SECTION.

❸ The macro processor sends the value of macro variable SECTION to the input stack. This value is treated as one token.

In Figure 5.19, all statements have been tokenized and macro variable references have been resolved. The macro program MYREPORT has terminated and the associated macro symbol table is deleted. The step is now ready to be executed.

Figure 5.19 The SAS program is ready for compilation

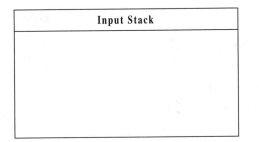

Input Stack

Word Scanner

| Tokenizer | Determine Destination of Token |

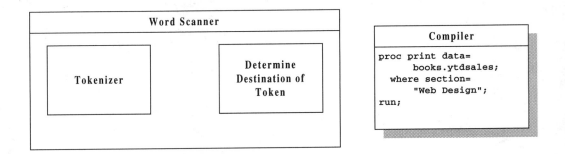

Compiler

```
proc print data=
     books.ytdsales;
  where section=
     "Web Design";
run;
```

Macro Processor

Global Macro Symbol Table

SAS Automatic Macro Variables
```
SYSDATE    11DEC98
SYSDAY     Friday
SYSVER     7.00
  .
  .
  .
```

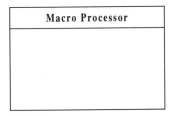

Macro Catalog

```
%macro myreport(section);
  %if &sysday=Friday %then %do;
    proc print data=books.ytdsales;
      where section="&section";
    run;
  %end;
%mend myreport;
```

CHAPTER 6

Macro Programming Language Elements and Techniques

The topics discussed so far can help you accomplish many SAS programming tasks. With the information that is presented in this chapter, you can learn how to delegate even more work to the macro processor.

The macro language contains functions and statements that can communicate complex instructions to the macro processor. Some of the statements, %LET, %PUT, and %MACRO, have already been described. Many of the macro functions and macro statements have SAS language counterparts. If you know how to write DATA step programs, you already have a familiarity with the style and structure of many of the macro functions and macro language statements.

This chapter describes macro language functions and macro language statements. Programming techniques with the macro language are also described in this chapter. The special topic of quoting is discussed.

Macro Language Functions

Macro functions greatly extend the use of macro variables and macro programming. The macro processor applies the function to the arguments of the macro function and returns a text value.

The arguments of a macro function can be text strings, macro variables, or macro functions. The result of a macro function is always text. This result can be assigned to a macro variable. A macro function can also be inserted directly into your SAS statements to build SAS statements.

Macro functions can be used in open code and in macro programs.

Some of the tasks you can do with macro functions include

- extracting substrings of macro variables

- searching for a string of characters in a macro variable

- temporarily converting macro values to numeric so that you can use the macro variables in calculations

- using SAS language functions and functions created with SAS/TOOLKIT in your macro language statements

- allowing semicolons to be treated as part of a macro variable value rather than as a symbol to terminate a statement.

The four types of macro functions—character, evaluation, quoting, and other—are briefly described below.

Macro Character Functions

Macro character functions operate on strings of characters or on macro variables. These functions modify their arguments or provide information about their arguments. Several of the character functions you may be familiar with in the SAS language have macro language counterparts. Macro character functions are listed in Table 6.1.

Table 6.1　Macro character functions

Function	Action
%INDEX(*source, string*)	returns the position in *source* of the first character of *string*
%LENGTH(*string/text expression*)	returns the length of *string* or the length of the results of the resolution of *text expression*
%SCAN(*argument, n <,delimiters>*) %QSCAN(*argument, n <,delimiters>*)	returns the nth word in *argument* where the words in *argument* are separated by *delimiters* does the same as %SCAN with the addition of masking special characters and mnemonic operators
%SUBSTR(*argument,position<,length>*) %QSUBSTR(*argument,position<,length>*)	extracts a substring of *length* characters from *argument* starting at *position* does the same as %SUBSTR with the addition of masking special characters and mnemonic operators
%UPCASE(*string/text expression*) %QUPCASE(*string/text expression*)	converts *character string* or *text expression* to upper case does the same as %UPCASE with the addition of masking special characters and mnemonic operators

Example: Using the %SUBSTR Macro Character Function

The next example shows how the %SUBSTR function extracts text from strings of characters. The WHERE statement selects observations from the first day of the current month through the day the program was run.

```
proc means data=book.ytdsales;
   title "Sales for %substr(&sysdate,3,3) through &sysdate";
   where "01%substr(&sysdate,3)"d le datesold le "&sysdate"d;
   class section;
   var salepric;
run;
```

After resolution of the macro variable references, the PROC MEANS step looks as follows when submitted on September 11, 1998.

```
proc means data=book.ytdsales;
   title "Sales for SEP through 11SEP98";
   where "01SEP98"d le datesold le "11SEP98"d;
   class section;
   var salepric;
run;
```

Example: Using the %SCAN Macro Character Function

The next example uses the %SCAN macro character function to extract a specific word from a string of words. In this example, the request is to extract the third word, specified by the value of REPMONTH, from the macro variable MONTHS.

```
%let months=January February March April May June;
%let repmonth=3;

proc print data=books.ytdsales;
   title "Sales Report for %scan(&months,&repmonth)";
   where month(datesold)=&repmonth;
   var title author salepric;
run;
```

After resolution of the macro variable references, the PROC PRINT step looks like this:

```
proc print data=books.ytdsales;
   title "Sales Report for March";
   where month(datesold)=3;
   var title author salepric;
run;
```

Example: Using the %UPCASE Macro Character Function

The next macro program lists all the titles containing a specific text string that have been sold. The text string is passed to the macro program through the parameter KEYTEXT. This text string may be in different forms in the title: lower case, upper case, mixed case. Because of this, both the macro variable's value and the value of the data set variable TITLE are converted to upper case. Now all combinations are found when the two are compared.

```
%macro listtext(keytext);
  %let keytext=%upcase(&keytext);
  proc print data=books.ytdsales;
  title "Book Titles Sold Containing Text String &keytext";
    where index(upcase(title),"&keytext") > 0;
    var title author salepric;
  run;
%mend;

%listtext(web)
```

When the macro program executes, the TITLE statement resolves to

```
Book Titles Sold Containing Text String WEB
```

The WHERE statement at execution resolves to

```
where index(upcase(title),"WEB") > 0;
```

The KEYTEXT macro variable reference in the WHERE statement in the macro program is enclosed in double quotation marks. The double quotation marks serve two purposes in this SAS language statement:

1. Double quotation marks around a macro variable reference allow the macro variable to be resolved. A macro variable reference that is enclosed in single quotation marks will not be resolved.

2. Quotation marks, single or double, are required around the text string that is processed by the SAS language functions INDEX and UPCASE.

Macro Evaluation Functions

Macro evaluation functions evaluate arithmetic expressions or logical expressions. The arguments of a macro evaluation function are temporarily converted to numbers so that a calculation can be done. The result of a macro evaluation function is converted back to text.

There are two evaluation functions: %EVAL and %SYSEVALF. The %EVAL function evaluates expressions using integer arithmetic; the %SYSEVALF function evaluates expressions using floating point arithmetic. The expressions are constructed with the same arithmetic and comparison operators found in the SAS language. Constructing expressions is described in more detail later in this chapter.

The syntax of the %EVAL function is

```
%EVAL(arithmetic expression|logical expression)
```

The syntax of the %SYSEVALF function is

```
%SYSEVALF(arithmetic expression|logical expression
    <,conversion-type>)
```

By default, the result of the %SYSEVALF function is left as a number which is converted back to text. In addition, %SYSEVALF can convert results to one of four types listed in Table 6.2.

Table 6.2   Conversion types that can be specified on the %SYSEVALF function

Conversion Type	Result that is returned by %SYSEVALF
BOOLEAN	0 if the result of the expression is 0 or missing 1 if the result is any other value (The 0 and 1 are treated as text.)
CEIL	text that represents the smallest integer that is greater than or equal to the result of the expression
FLOOR	text that represents the largest integer that is less than or equal to the result of the expression
INTEGER	text that represents the integer portion of the result of the expression

The %EVAL function does integer arithmetic; numbers with decimal points are treated as text. The %EVAL function generates an error when there are characters in the arguments that are supplied to %EVAL.

The statements in Table 6.3 show examples of the %EVAL and %SYSEVALF functions. The %PUT statements were submitted and the results were written to the SAS log.

Table 6.3   Examples of %EVAL and %SYSEVALF evaluation functions

%PUT Statement	Results in SAS log
`%put %eval(33 + 44);`	77
`%put %eval(33.2 + 44.1);`	ERROR: A character operand was found in the %EVAL function or %IF condition where a numeric operand is required. The condition was: 33.2 + 44.1
`%put %sysevalf(33.2 + 44.1);`	77.3
`%put %sysevalf(33.2 + 44.1,integer);`	77
`%let a=3;` `%let b=10;`	
`%put %eval(&b/&a);`	3
`%put %sysevalf(&b/&a);`	3.3333333333
`%put %sysevalf(&b/&a,ceil);`	4
`%put %sysevalf(&b/&a,boolean);`	1
`%let missvalu=.;`	
`%put %sysevalf(&b-&missvalu,boolean);`	NOTE: Missing values were generated as a result of performing an operation on missing values during %SYSEVALF expression evaluation. 0

Macro Quoting Functions

Macro quoting functions mask special characters and mnemonic operators in your macro language statements so that the macro processor ignores them and does not interpret them. Macro quoting functions are described more fully later in this chapter in the section on masking characters and operators.

Other Macro Functions

The four macro functions described in this section do not fit into any of the three categories of macro functions described so far. These four functions do one of the following:

- apply SAS language functions to macro variables or text

- obtain information from the rest of the SAS System or the operating system in which the SAS session is running.

The four macro functions are listed in Table 6.4.

Table 6.4   Other macro functions

Function	Action
%SYSFUNC (*function(argument(s))* <*,format*>)	executes SAS language *function* or user-written *function* and returns the results to the macro facility (see also macro statement %SYSCALL)
%QSYSFUNC (*function(argument(s))* <*,format*>)	does the same as %SYSFUNC with the addition of masking special characters and mnemonic operators in the *argument(s)*
%SYSGET (*host-environment-variable*)	returns the value of *host-environment-variable* to the macro facility
%SYSPROD (*SAS-product*)	returns a code to indicate whether *SAS-product* is licensed at the site where the SAS System is currently running

Using the %SYSFUNC and %QSYSFUNC Macro Functions

The functions %SYSFUNC and %QSYSFUNC apply SAS programming language functions to text and macro variables in your macro programming. Since %SYSFUNC is a macro function and the macro facility is a text handling language, the arguments to the SAS programming language function are not enclosed in quotation marks; it is understood that all arguments are text.

Functions cannot be nested within one call to %SYSFUNC. Each function must have its own %SYSFUNC call and these %SYSFUNC calls can be nested.

Example: Using the %SYSFUNC Function to Format a TITLE Statement

As an example of the formatting capabilities of %SYSFUNC, a TITLE statement is customized as follows:

```
title
   "Sales for %sysfunc(date(),monname.) %sysfunc(date(),year.)";
```

On January 30, 1998, the title statement would resolve to

```
Sales for January 1998
```

Example: Using the %SYSFUNC Function to Apply a SAS Language Function

Another example of using %SYSFUNC follows. This time %SYSFUNC is used to obtain information from the SAS language function GETOPTION. GETOPTION displays SAS System options. The option name that GETOPTION is to check is passed to the macro program as a parameter.

```
%macro getopt(whatopt);
   %let optvalue=%sysfunc(getoption(&whatopt));
   %put Option &whatopt = &optvalue;
%mend getopt;

%getopt(ps)
%getopt(ls)
%getopt(date)
%getopt(symbolgen)
%getopt(compress)
```

After the above code is submitted, the following is written to the SAS log:

```
58    %getopt(ps)
Option ps = 54
59    %getopt(ls)
Option ls = 90
60    %getopt(date)
Option date = DATE
61    %getopt(symbolgen)
Option symbolgen = NOSYMBOLGEN
62    %getopt(compress)
Option compress = NO
```

Example: Using the %SYSFUNC Function to Apply Several SAS Language Functions that Obtain Information about a Data Set

This next example uses %SYSFUNC to obtain the number of observations in a data set and store that number in a macro variable. First the data set is opened with the SAS language OPEN function. Then the SAS language ATTRN function obtains the number of observations and stores the value in the macro variable NOBS. Finally, the SAS language CLOSE function closes the data set.

```
%let dsid=%sysfunc(open(books.ytdsales));
%let nobs=%sysfunc(attrn(&dsid,nobs));
%let rc=%sysfunc(close(&dsid));

proc means data=books.ytdsales sum maxdec=2;
   title "Year-to-Date Sales Report: &sysdate";
   title2 "Number of Books Sold: &nobs";
   class section;
   var salepric;
run;
```

The output for the above program is in Figure 6.1.

Figure 6.1   Output for program with %SYSFUNC macro interface function

```
         Year-to-Date Sales Report: 31JUL98                1
              Number of Books Sold: 3778
                             14:52 Friday, July 31, 1998


    Analysis Variable : SALEPRIC Sale Price


    SECTION                      N Obs          Sum
    ------------------------------------------------
    Internet                       973     29666.46

    Networks and Communication     361     10706.75

    Operating Systems             1029     31274.40

    Programming Languages          486     14447.24

    Web Design                     929     28303.18
    ------------------------------------------------
```

Macro Language Statements

Macro language statements communicate your instructions to the macro processor. With macro language statements, you can write macro programs that conditionally or repetitively execute sections of code.

Many macro language statements have a SAS language counterpart. The syntax and function of similarly named statements are the same.

Remember, however, that macro language statements *build* SAS programs and are processed before the SAS programs they build. Macro language statements are *not* part of the DATA step programming language. They operate in a different context. They *write* SAS programs.

Macro language statements can be grouped into two types:

- statements that can be used either in open code or inside a macro program

- statements that can only be used inside a macro program.

The following two tables list most of the macro language statements. Some are shown by example in this chapter; more are described in the dictionary. Detailed reference information on these statements is in *SAS Macro Language: Reference*.

As an aid in remembering the type of a macro language statement, observe that the statements in Table 6.5 work on macro variables or act as definition type statements. These statements can be used either in open code or inside a macro program.

On the other hand, most of the macro language statements in Table 6.6 are active programming statements that control processing and work in conjunction with other statements. These statements can only be used inside a macro program.

Table 6.5   Macro language statements that can be used either in open code or inside a macro program

Statement	Action
%* comment;	adds descriptive text to your macro code.
%GLOBAL	creates macro variables that are stored in the global symbol table and will be available throughout the SAS session.
%KEYDEF	assigns a definition, such as a string of SAS commands, to a function key.
%LET	creates a macro variable and/or assigns it a value.
%MACRO	begins the definition of a macro program.
%PUT	writes text or macro variable values to the SAS log.
%SYSCALL	invokes a SAS System or user-written call routine using macro variables as the arguments and generating text as the result; operates in the macro processing domain. (see also the %SYSFUNC macro function).
%SYSEXEC	executes operating system commands immediately in the macro domain.
%SYSRPUT	assigns the value of a macro variable on a remote host to a macro variable on the local host. Used with SAS/CONNECT.

Table 6.6 lists the macro language statements that can only be used inside a macro program.

Table 6.6   Macro language statements that can only be used inside a macro program

Statement	Action
%DO	signals the beginning of a %DO group; the statements that follow form a block of code that is terminated with a %END statement.
%DO, iterative	repetitively executes a section of macro code by using an index variable and the keywords %TO and %BY; the section of macro code is terminated with a %END statement.
%DO %UNTIL	repetitively executes a section of macro code *until* the macro expression that follows the %UNTIL is true; the section of macro code is terminated with a %END statement.
%DO %WHILE	repetitively executes a section of macro code *while* the macro expression that follows the %WHILE is true; the section of macro code is terminated with a %END statement.
%END	terminates a %DO group.
%GOTO	branches macro processing to the specified macro label within the macro program.
%IF-%THEN %ELSE	conditionally processes the section of macro code that follows the %THEN when the result of the macro expression that follows %IF is true; when the macro expression that follows %IF is false, the section of macro code that follows the %ELSE is executed.
%label:	identifies a section of macro code; typically used as the destination of a %GOTO statement.
%LOCAL	creates macro variables that are available only to the macro program in which the %LOCAL statement was issued.
%MEND	ends a macro program that was created with a %MACRO statement

Constructing Macro Language Expressions

Expressions in the macro language are constructed similarly to expressions in the SAS programming language. The same arithmetic and logical operators are used in both macro expressions and SAS language expressions. The exceptions to this are that the MAX operator, the MIN operator, the IN operator, and the ':' symbol are not available in the macro language. The same precedence rules also apply. Parentheses act to group expressions and control the order of evaluation of expressions.

Table 6.7 lists the operators in order of precedence of evaluation. The symbols for the NOT and NE operators depend on your computer system. Do not place percent signs in front of the mnemonic operators.

Table 6.7   Arithmetic and logical operators and their precedence in the macro language

Operator	Mnemonic	Action	Precedence Rating
**		exponentiation	1
+		positive prefix	2
-		negative prefix	2
^	NOT	logical not	3
*		multiplication	4
/		division	4
+		addition	5
-		subtraction	5
<	LT	less than	6
<=	LE	less than or equal to	6
=	EQ	equal	6
^=	NE	not equal	6
>	GT	greater than	6
>=	GE	greater than or equal to	6
&	AND	logical and	7
|	OR	logical or	8

Arithmetic Expressions

Since the macro language is a text based language, working with numbers is the exception. Special considerations are needed when you are writing expressions that use numbers.

Several of the macro language statements and functions require numeric or logical expressions. These elements automatically invoke the %EVAL function to convert the expressions from text.

Macro evaluation functions, described earlier in this chapter, temporarily convert their arguments to numbers in order to resolve arithmetic expressions.

The macro functions that automatically invoke %EVAL around the arguments supplied to them are

- %SUBSTR and %QSUBSTR

- %SCAN and %QSCAN.

The macro language statements that automatically invoke %EVAL around the arguments supplied to them are

- %DO

- %DO %UNTIL

- %DO %WHILE

- %IF.

Therefore, when you use these functions and statements, explicitly coding the %EVAL function around the macro arithmetic expression is redundant.

Refer to the section on macro evaluation functions for examples of arithmetic macro expressions. More examples of expressions follow throughout the description of macro language statements.

Logical Expressions

A logical expression in the macro language compares two macro expressions. These macro expressions consist of text, macro variables, macro functions, arithmetic expressions, and other logical expressions. If the comparison is true, the result is a value of one. If the comparison is false, the result is zero. Expressions that resolve to integers other than zero are also considered true. Expressions that resolve to zero are false.

The comparison operators in Table 6.7 construct logical expressions in the macro language.

As the macro processor resolves a macro expression, it places a %EVAL around each of the operands in the expression to temporarily convert the operands to integers. If an operand cannot be an integer, the macro facility then treats all operands in the expression as text. Comparisons are then based on the sort sequence of characters in the host operating system.

When you want numbers with decimal points to be compared as numbers and not compared as text, place the %SYSEVALF function around the logical expression.

The %SYSEVALF function with the BOOLEAN conversion type acts like a logical expression because it yields a true-false result of one or zero.

Logical expressions are used in conditional processing. Examples of logical expressions and conditional processing are provided in the next section.

Conditional Processing with the Macro Language

A basic feature of any programming language is conditional execution of code. The macro language uses %IF-%THEN/%ELSE statements to control execution of sections of code. The sections of code that can be selected include macro language statements or text.

Remember that text in the macro facility can be SAS language statements like DATA steps and PROC steps. Thus, within your macro programs, based on evaluation of conditions you set, you can direct the macro processor to submit specific SAS statements for execution. With this capability, one macro program can contain many SAS language statements and steps and be used repeatedly to manage various processing tasks.

The syntax of the %IF statement is

```
%IF expression %THEN action;
<%ELSE elseaction;>
```

Multiple %ELSE statements can be specified to test for multiple conditions.

The expression that you write is usually a logical expression. The macro processor invokes the %EVAL function around the expression and resolves the expression to true or false. When the evaluation of the expression is true, *action* is executed. When the evaluation of the expression is false and an %ELSE statement is specified, *elseaction* is executed.

Example: Using Logical Expressions

The next macro program illustrates evaluation of logical expressions. There are three calls to the macro program COMPARES. Four comparisons of the two parameters are made with each call to COMPARES.

```
%macro compares(value1,value2);
  %put COMPARISON 1:;
  %if &value1 ne &value2 %then
    %put &value1 is not equal to &value2..;
  %else %put &value1 equals &value2..;

  %put COMPARISON 2:;
  %if &value1 > &value2 %then
    %put &value1 is greater than &value2..;
  %else %if &value1 < &value2 %then
    %put &value1 is less than &value2..;
  %else %put &value1 equals &value2..;

  %put COMPARISON 3:;
  %let result=%eval(&value1 > &value2);
  %if &result=1 %then
    %put EVAL result of &value1 > &value2 is TRUE.;
  %else %put EVAL result of &value1 > &value2 is FALSE.;

  %put COMPARISON 4:;
  %let result=%sysevalf(&value1 > &value2);
  %if &result=1 %then
    %put SYSEVALF result of &value1 > &value2 is TRUE.;
  %else %put SYSEVALF result of &value1 > &value2 is FALSE.;

%mend compares;

*----First call to COMPARES;
%compares(3,4)

*----Second call to COMPARES;
%compares(3.0,3)

*----Third call to COMPARES;
%compares(X,x)
```

The SAS log for %COMPARES(3,4) follows.

```
63   %compares(3,4)
COMPARISON 1:
3 is not equal to 4
COMPARISON 2:
3 is less than 4.
COMPARISON 3:
EVAL result of 3 > 4 is FALSE.
COMPARISON 4:
SYSEVALF result of 3 > 4 is FALSE.
```

The SAS log for %COMPARES(3.0,3) follows.

```
65   %compares(3.0,3)
COMPARISON 1:
```

```
3.0 is not equal to 3
COMPARISON 2:
3.0 is greater than 3.
COMPARISON 3:
EVAL result of 3.0 > 3 is TRUE.
COMPARISON 4:
SYSEVALF result of 3.0 > 3 is FALSE.
```

The SAS log for % COMPARES(X,x) follows.

```
67   %compares(X,x)
COMPARISON 1:
X is not equal to x.
COMPARISON 2:
X is less than x.
COMPARISON 3:
EVAL result of X > x is FALSE.
COMPARISON 4:
SYSEVALF result of X > x is FALSE.
```

Example: Using Macro Language Statements to Select SAS Steps for Processing

The next program is an example of how you can instruct the macro processor to select certain SAS steps. The type of the report to be produced is specified as a parameter to the macro program REPORT. The choices are SUMMARY or DETAIL. The other parameter, REPMONTH, is the month for which the report is produced.

The macro program is called twice. The first call to REPORTS requests a summary report for September. When a summary report is requested, the first PROC TABULATE step is selected. When REPORTS is processed for the last month in a quarter, the second PROC TABULATE step is selected.

The second call to REPORTS requests a detail report for October. When a detail report is specified, the PROC PRINT step is executed for the specified month.

```
%macro reports(reptype,repmonth);
  %let lblmonth=
    %sysfunc(mdy(&repmonth,1,%substr(&sysdate,6,2)),monname.);

  %*----Begin summary report section;
  %if %upcase(&reptype)=SUMMARY %then %do;
    %*----Do summary report for report month;
    proc tabulate data=books.ytdsales;
      title "Sales for &lblmonth";
      where month(datesold)=&repmonth;
      class section;
```

```
      var listpric salepric;
      tables section,
         (listpric salepric)*(n*f=6. sum*f=dollar12.2);
   run;
   %*----If end of quarter, also do summary report for qtr;
   %if &repmonth=3 or &repmonth=6 or &repmonth=9
      or &repmonth=12 %then %do;
      %let qtrstart=%eval(&repmonth-2);

      %let strtmo=
      %sysfunc(mdy(&qtrstart,1,%substr(&sysdate,6,2)),monname.);

      proc tabulate data=books.ytdsales;
         title "Sales for Quarter from &strtmo to &lblmonth";
         where &strtmo le month(datesold) le &repmonth;
         class section;
         var listpric salepric;
         tables section,
            (listpric salepric)*(n*f=6. sum*f=dollar12.2);
      run;
   %end;
%end;
   %*----End summary report section;
   %*----Begin detail report section;
%else %if %upcase(&reptype)=DETAIL %then %do;
   %*----Do detail report for month;
   proc print data=books.ytdsales;
      where month(datesold)=&repmonth;
      var title cost listpric salepric;
      sum cost listpric salepric;
   run;
%end;
   %*----End detail report section;
%mend reports;

*----First call to REPORTS does a Summary report for September;
%reports(Summary,9)

*----Second call to REPORTS does a Detail report for October;
%reports(Detail,10)
```

The first call to REPORTS specifies summary reports for September. The following code is selected from the macro program and is shown after resolution of the macro variables.

```
proc tabulate data=books.ytdsales;
   title "Sales for September";
   where month(datesold)=9;
   class section;
   var listpric salepric;
   tables section,(listpric salepric)*(n*f=6. sum*f=dollar12.2);
run;
```

```
proc tabulate data=books.ytdsales;
   title "Sales for Quarter from July to September";
   where 7 le month(datesold) le 9;
   class section;
   var listpric salepric;
   tables section,(listpric salepric)*(n*f=6. sum*f=dollar12.2);
run;
```

The second call to REPORT specifies the detail report for October. After macro variable resolution, the following code is selected.

```
proc print data=books.ytdsales;
   where month(datesold)=10;
   var title cost listpric salepric;
   sum cost listpric salepric;
run;
```

Example: Using %IF-%THEN/%ELSE Statements to Modify and Select Statements within a Step

The last example in this section shows how %IF-%THEN/%ELSE statements can select the statements within a step. This example also illustrates the timing of processing of macro language statements and SAS language statements.

As we've seen before, macro language statements are the instructions that the macro processor takes from you to build your SAS programs. After the macro processor is done, the word scanner takes over to tokenize the SAS statements that the macro processor has built. So, the %IF-%THEN/%ELSE statements in this example operate before the SAS steps are tokenized, compiled, and executed.

The parameter to the SALES macro program is a classification variable. When the parameter is specified, the PROC TABULATE report contains information that is based on the values of the classification variable. The classification variable is the row dimension variable in the TABULATE table. Also, a PROC SORT is done so that the PROC UNIVARIATE analysis is displayed in groups defined by the values of the classification variable.

When the parameter is not specified, an overall summary is produced by PROC TABULATE and PROC UNIVARIATE. PROC SORT is not invoked.

The SALES macro program is called twice: once to process the reports by a classification variable and once to process the reports overall.

```
%macro sales(classvar);
   title "Sales Year-to-Date";
   proc tabulate data=books.ytdsales;
```

```
   %*----When there is a classification variable, issue a;
   %*----CLASS statement;
   %if &classvar ne %then %do;
      class &classvar;
   %end;

   var listpric salepric;

   tables

   %*----When there is a classification variable, add the;
   %*----classification variable to the TABLES statement;
   %if &classvar ne %then %do;
       &classvar all,
   %end;

   (listpric salepric)*(n*f=5. sum*f=dollar12.2);
   run;

   %*----When there is a classification variable, call;
   %*----PROC SORT;
   %if &classvar ne %then %do;
      proc sort data=books.ytdsales;
         by &classvar;
      run;
   %end;

   %*----When there is a classification variable, issue a;
   %*----BY statement;
   proc univariate data=books.ytdsales;
      %if &classvar ne %then %do;
         by &classvar;
      %end;
      var listpric salepric;
   run;
%mend sales;

*----First call to SALES processes the data by section;
%sales(section)

*----Second call to SALES summarizes the data overall;
%sales()
```

The first call to SALES selects the following code. The program is shown after macro variable resolution.

```
title "Sales Year-to-Date";
proc tabulate data=books.ytdsales;
   class section;
   var listpric salepric;
   tables
      section all,
```

```
       (listpric salepric)*(n*f=5. sum*f=dollar12.2);
run;

proc sort data=books.ytdsales;
  by section;
run;

proc univariate data=books.ytdsales;
  by section;
  var listpric salepric;
run;
```

The second call produces the following SAS program after macro variable resolution.

```
title "Sales Year-to-Date";
proc tabulate data=books.ytdsales;
  var listpric salepric;
  tables
  (listpric salepric)*(n*f=5. sum*f=dollar12.2);
run;

proc univariate data=books.ytdsales;
  var listpric salepric;
run;
```

Iterative Processing with the Macro Language

The iterative processing statements in the macro language instruct the macro processor to repetitively process sections of code. The macro language includes %DO loops, %DO %UNTIL blocks, and %DO %WHILE blocks. With iterative processing, you can instruct the macro processor to write many SAS language statements, DATA steps, and PROC steps. The three types of iterative processing statements are described below. These statements may only be used from within a macro program.

Writing Iterative %DO Loops in the Macro Language

The iterative %DO macro language statement instructs the macro processor to execute repetitively a section of code. The number of times the section is executed is based on the value of an index variable. The index variable is a macro variable. You define the start value and stop value of the index variable. You can also control the increment of the steps between the start value and the stop value; by default the increment value is one.

The syntax of an iterative %DO loop is as follows.

```
%DO macro-variable=start %TO stop <%BY increment>;
  macro language statements and/or text
%END;
```

Do not put an ampersand in front of the index variable name in the %DO statement even though the index variable is a macro variable. Any reference to it later within the loop, however, requires an ampersand in front of the reference.

The start and stop values are integers or macro expressions that can be resolved to integers. If you want to increment the index macro variable by something other than one, follow the stop value with the %BY keyword and the increment value. The increment value is either an integer or a macro expression that can be resolved to an integer.

Example: Using the Iterative %DO Macro Statement to Build PROC Steps

The following example uses the iterative %DO to generate several PROC MEANS and PROC GCHART steps. This macro program generates statistics and a bar chart for each year between the bounds on the %DO statement. In this example, PROC MEANS and PROC GCHART are each executed three times: once for 1997, once for 1998 and once for 1999.

```
%macro multrep(strtyear,stopyear);
   %do yrvalue=&strtyear %to &stopyear;
      title "Sales Report for &yrvalue";
      proc means data=sales.year&yrvalue;
        class section;
        var cost listpric salepric;
      run;

      proc gchart data=sales.year&yrvalue;
        hbar section / sumvar=salepric type=sum;
      run;
      quit;
   %end;
%mend multrep;

*----Produce 3 sets of reports: one for 1997, one for 1998,
*----and one for 1999;
%multrep(1997,1999)
```

After the macro processor processes the macro language statements and resolves the macro variables references, the following SAS program is submitted.

```
title "Sales Report for 1997";
proc means data=sales.year1997;
   class section;
   var cost listpric salepric;
run;
```

```
proc gchart data=sales.year1997;
  hbar section / sumvar=salepric type=sum;
run;

title "Sales Report for 1998";
proc means data=sales.year1998;
  class section;
  var cost listpric salepric;
run;

proc gchart data=sales.year1998;
  hbar section / sumvar=salepric type=sum;
run;

title "Sales Report for 1999";
proc means data=sales.year1999;
  class section;
  var cost listpric salepric;
run;

proc gchart data=sales.year1999;
  hbar section / sumvar=salepric type=sum;
run;
```

Example: Using the Iterative %DO Macro Statement to Build SAS Statements within a Step

Iterative %DO statements can build SAS statements within a SAS DATA step or SAS PROC step. The following example shows how several data sets can be concatenated in a DATA step.

Note that there is no semicolon after the reference to the data set within the %DO loop. If a semicolon was placed after the data set reference, then on the first iteration, the semicolon would terminate the SET statement. On each subsequent iteration, a semicolon after the data set reference would make the data set reference a SAS statement. This would result in errors.

```
%macro multchrt(strtyear,stopyear);
  data allyears;
    set
    %do yrvalue=&strtyear %to &stopyear;
      sales.year&yrvalue
    %end;
    ;
  run;

  %let yrstrng=;
  %do yrvalue=&strtyear %to &stopyear;
    %let yrstrng=&yrstrng &i;
  %end;
  proc gchart data=allyears;
    title "Charts Analyze Data for: &yrstrng";
```

```
      hbar section / sumvar=salepric type=sum;
   run;
%mend multchrt;

*----Concatenate three data sets: one from 1997, one from 1998,
*----and one from 1999;
%multchrt(1997,1999)
```

The macro processor resolves the call to MULTCHRT as follows.

```
data allyears;
   set sales.year1997 sales.year1998 sales.year1999;
run;

proc gchart data=allyears;
   title "Charts Analyze Data for: 1997 1998 1999";
   hbar section / sumvar=salepric type=sum;
run;
```

Conditional Iteration with %DO %UNTIL

With %DO %UNTIL, a section of code is executed *until* the condition on the %DO %UNTIL statement is true. The syntax of %DO %UNTIL is

```
%DO %UNTIL (expression);
   macro language statements and/or text
%END;
```

The expression on the %DO %UNTIL statement is a macro expression that resolves to a true-false value. The macro processor evaluates the expression at the bottom of each iteration. Therefore, a %DO %UNTIL block always executes at least once.

Example: Using the %DO %UNTIL Macro Statements

An example of using %DO %UNTIL follows. The macro program MOSALES computes statistics for each of the months passed to the program in the parameter MONTHS. If no months are specified, an overall PROC MEANS is done. This overall PROC MEANS is accomplished by taking advantage of the features of %DO %UNTIL. A %DO %UNTIL block is executed at least once.

```
%macro mosales(months);
   %let i=1;
   %do %until (%scan(&months,&i) eq );
      %let repmonth=%scan(&months,&i);
      proc means data=books.ytdsales n sum;
         %if &repmonth ne %then %do;
            title "Sales during month &repmonth";
```

```
        where month(datesold)=&repmonth;
      %end;
      %else %do;
        title "Overall Sales";
      %end;
      class section;
      var salepric;
    run;
    %let i=%eval(&i+1);
  %end;
%mend;

*----First call to MOSALES: produce stats for March, May, and
*----October;
%mosales(3 5 10)

*----Second call to MOSALES: produce overall stats;
%mosales()
```

The first call to MOSALES requests statistics for March, May, and October. The macro processor generates the following SAS program.

```
proc means data=books.ytdsales n sum;
  title "Sales during month 3";
  where month(datesold)=3;
  class section;
  var salepric;
run;
proc means data=books.ytdsales n sum;
  title "Sales during month 5";
  where month(datesold)=5;
  class section;
  var salepric;
run;
proc means data=books.ytdsales n sum;
  title "Sales during month 10";
  where month(datesold)=10;
  class section;
  var salepric;
run;
```

The second call to MOSALES does not specify any months. Therefore, the %DO %UNTIL block is executed once and generates overall statistics. The SAS program that the macro processor creates from this call follows:

```
proc means data=books.ytdsales n sum;
  title "Overall Sales";
  class section;
  var salepric;
run;
```

Conditional Iteration with %DO %WHILE

With %DO %WHILE, a section of code is executed *while* the condition on the %DO %WHILE statement is true. The syntax of %DO %WHILE is as follows:

```
%DO %WHILE (expression);
  macro language statements and/or text
%END;
```

The expression on the %DO %WHILE statement is a macro expression that resolves to a true-false value. The macro processor evaluates the expression at the top of the loop. Therefore, it is possible that a %DO %WHILE block will not execute. This happens when the condition starts out as false.

Example: Using the %DO %WHILE Macro Language Statements

An example of using %DO %WHILE follows. Sales reports are generated for three sales representatives during May.

```
%macro staff(reps,repmonth);
  %let i=1;
  %do %while (%scan(&reps,&i) ne );
    %let inits=%scan(&reps,&i);
    proc means data=books.ytdsales n sum;
      title "Sales for &inits during month &repmonth";
      where saleinit="&inits" and month(datesold)=&repmonth;
      class section;
      var salepric;
    run;
    %let i=%eval(&i+1);
  %end;
%mend;

%staff(MJM BLT JMB,5)
```

After resolution by the macro processor, the SAS code submitted for compilation and execution is as follows. Three PROC MEANS steps are created: one for each of the three sales representative.

```
proc means data=books.ytdsales n sum;
  title "Sales for MJM during month 5";
  where saleinit="MJM" and month(datesold)=5;
  class section;
  var salepric;
run;

proc means data=books.ytdsales n sum;
  title "Sales for BLT during month 5";
  where saleinit="BLT" and month(datesold)=5;
```

```
   class section;
   var salepric;
run;

proc means data=books.ytdsales n sum;
   title "Sales for JMB during month 5";
   where saleinit="JMB" and month(datesold)=5;
   class section;
   var salepric;
run;
```

Branching in Macro Processing

When you want to branch to a different section of a macro program, label the text and use a %GOTO statement. The %GOTO statement directs processing to that labelled text. Labelled text and the %GOTO statement are only allowed in macro programs. Macro language statements, macro expressions, and constant text can be labelled. Macro text is labelled as follows:

```
%label: macro-text
```

Place the label preceding the macro text you want to identify. The label is any valid SAS name. Precede the label with a percent sign (%) and follow the label name with a colon (:).

The syntax of the %GOTO statement is

```
%GOTO label;
```

On the %GOTO statement, the label can be specified as text or as a macro expression. Do not put a percent sign in front of the label on the %GOTO statement. If you do specify a percent sign, the macro processor interprets that as a request to execute a macro program that has the name of your label.

Example: Using the %GOTO Macro Language Statement

The following example shows how labels and %GOTO statements can be used. If the data set specified in the parameter DSNAME exists, a PROC PRINT step is executed. If the data set does not exist, the program branches to the code identified with the %NODATA label. A message is written to the SAS log and the PROC DATASETS step is selected.

```
%macro detail(dsname,listvars);
   %let foundit=%sysfunc(exist(&dsname));
   %if &foundit le 0 %then %goto nodata;

   title "PROC PRINT of &dsname";
   proc print data=&dsname;
     var &listvars;
```

```
run;
%goto finished;

%nodata:
    %put **** Data set &dsname not found. ****;
    proc datasets library=books details;
    run;
    quit;

%finished:
%mend;

*----First call to DETAIL, data set exists;
%detail(books.ytdsales,saledate title salepric)

*----Second call to DETAIL, data set does not exist;
%detail(boooks.ytdsales,saledate title salepric)
```

The first call to the macro program DETAIL produces a PROC PRINT for the data set and the variables specified in the parameters. The section labelled as %NODATA is skipped, and the macro processor generates the following code:

```
title "PROC PRINT of books.ytdsales";
proc print data=books.ytdsales;
    var saledate title salepric;
run;
```

The data set name is misspelled in the second call to DETAIL. A data set with this misspelled name does not exist. Now the PROC PRINT section is skipped and the section labelled with %NODATA is executed. The macro processor writes a message to the SAS log that the data set BOOOKS.YTDSALES does not exist. The following PROC DATASETS code is submitted.

```
proc datasets library=books details;
    run;
quit;
```

Masking Characters in the Macro Facility

The macro language does exactly what you tell it to do (sometimes unfortunately!). When the macro processor sees certain symbols like semicolons, percent signs, and ampersands or when it sees certain mnemonic operators like AND and OR in your macro language statements, it takes specific, unvarying actions.

The question that then may arise is whether you can tell the macro processor to ignore these special characters and mnemonic operators and instead treat them as text. For instance, what would happen if you set the code for an entire PROC step to a macro variable? The PROC step contains semicolons terminating the SAS language statements in the step. However, the macro processor treats the first semicolon it encounters as termination of the macro variable assignment, not termination of the first statement in the PROC step. Therefore, the macro variable does not contain all the information you wanted it to have. The SAS System proceeds to compile the remaining PROC step statements which did not become part of the macro variable's values. This likely results in execution errors.

The next statement is in error. Only the PROC statement is assigned to the macro variable WONTWORK.

```
%let wontwork=proc print data=books.ytdsales;var salepric;run;
```

The next statement handles the problems with the statement above. It uses a macro quoting function to prevent the macro processor from seeing the semicolons in the PROC step statements. Now all three PROC step statements are assigned to WILLWORK.

```
%let willwork=%str(proc print data=books.ytdsales;var
salepric;run;);
```

To prevent the macro processor from interpreting these special characters and mnemonic operators, use macro quoting functions. These functions mask special characters from view so that they are treated strictly as text by the macro processor.

In science fiction terms, macro quoting functions are the "cloaking device" of the macro facility.

Why are Quoting Functions called Quoting Functions?

The macro functions that mask special characters and mnemonic operators are called quoting functions because they behave like single quotation marks in the SAS language. Just as characters enclosed in single quotation marks in a SAS language statement are ignored, so are the arguments to a macro quoting function. The difference is that the macro quoting functions offer much more flexibility in what characters to ignore and when to ignore them.

Types of Macro Quoting Functions

The macro quoting functions can be grouped into three types based upon when they act: compilation, execution, and preventing resolution.

The two compilation functions, %STR and %NRSTR, mask special characters at the time of compilation. This means special characters in the arguments to these functions are treated as text during compilation. Typically one of these functions is used when you want to assign special characters to a macro variable.

The two execution functions, %BQUOTE and %NRBQUOTE, mask special characters that result from resolving macro expressions. Macro expressions are resolved during execution. These functions prevent special characters and mnemonic operators that are in arithmetic and logical expressions from being interpreted. These functions are typically used when working with %EVAL or %SYSEVALF or when working with statements and functions that automatically invoke %EVAL.

The one function that prevents resolution, %SUPERQ, masks the value of a macro variable so that the value is treated solely as text. Percent signs(%) and ampersands(&) in the value of a macro variable are not resolved.

The Characters and Operators that the Macro Quoting Functions Mask

The special characters and mnemonic operators that the macro functions can mask are listed in Table 6.8. An example of masking follows each description.

Table 6.8   The special characters and mnemonic operators that can be masked by macro quoting functions

Special Character / Mnemonic Operator	Reason for masking

;	to prevent interpretation of the semicolon as termination of a macro statement
	`%let myproc=%str(`
	`proc print data=books.ytdsales;var`
	`salepric;run;);`

,	to prevent interpretation of the comma as a delimiter for arguments to a function or macro program call `%let month=%substr( %str(Jan,Feb,Mar,),4,3);`

blank	to maintain blanks and not trim them from a string
	`%let titltext=`
	`%str(  B  o  o  k  S  a  l  e  s );`

+-*/<>=^|~&|^
LE LT EQ GT GE
NE
AND OR NOT
	to prevent the operator from being evaluated as an operator in a macro expression
	`%let state=OR;`
	`%let value=%sysevalf(`
	`    %bquote(&state) eq %bquote(OR), boolean);`

% &	to prevent resolution of a macro variable, macro statement or macro program `%let reptext=%nrstr( Jan&Feb %Sales Report );`

' " ( )	to allow use of unmatched pairs of quotation marks and parentheses
	`%let`
	`names=%bquote(O'DONOVAN,O'HARA,O'MALLEY);`
	`%let name3=%qscan(&names,3);`

Following are the statements in Table 6.8 with and without use of macro quoting functions. %PUT statements are included to list the values of the macro variables when macro quoting functions are used and not used.

Example: Using Macro Quoting Functions to Mask Semicolons

This example is for the semicolon (;).

```
%let myproc=proc print data=books.ytdsales;var salepric;run;
%put WITHOUT Quoting Functions MYPROC=&myproc;

%let myproc=%str(proc print data=books.ytdsales;var
salepric;run;);
%put WITH Quoting Functions MYPROC=&myproc;
```

The SAS log for the statements above follows.

```
6      %let myproc=proc print data=books.ytdsales;var salepric;
                                                           ---
                                                           180


ERROR 180-322: Statement is not valid or it is used out of
proper order.

6
run;
7      %put WITHOUT Quoting Functions MYPROC=&myproc;
WITHOUT Quoting Functions MYPROC=proc print data=books.ytdsales
8
9      %let myproc=%str(proc print data=books.ytdsales;var
salepric;run;);
10     %put WITH Quoting Functions MYPROC=&myproc;
WITH Quoting Functions MYPROC=proc print data=books.ytdsales;
var salepric;run;
```

Example: Using Macro Quoting Functions to Mask Commas

This example is for the comma (,).

```
%let month=%substr( Jan,Feb,Mar,5,3);
%put WITHOUT Quoting Functions MONTH=&month;
%let month=%substr( %str(Jan,Feb,Mar,),5,3);
%put WITH Quoting Functions MONTH=&month;
```

The SAS log for the previous statements looks like this:

```
ERROR: Macro function %SUBSTR has too many arguments.  The
excess arguments will be
```

```
            ignored.
ERROR: A character operand was found in the %EVAL function or
%IF condition where a
            numeric operand is required. The condition was: Feb
ERROR: Argument 2 to macro function %substr is not a number.
11    %let month=%substr( Jan,Feb,Mar,5,3);
12    %put WITHOUT Quoting Functions MONTH=&month;
WITHOUT Quoting Functions MONTH=
13    %let month=%substr( %str(Jan,Feb,Mar,),5,3);
14    %put WITH Quoting Functions MONTH=&month;
WITH Quoting Functions MONTH=Feb
```

Example: Using Macro Quoting Functions to Maintain Blanks in a String

This example is for the blanks.

```
%let titltext=    B  o  o  k    S  a  l  e  s ;
%put WITHOUT Quoting Functions TITLTEXT=&titltext;
%let titltext=%str(    B  o  o  k    S  a  l  e  s );
%put WITH Quoting Functions TITLTEXT=&titltext;
```

The SAS log for the previous statements looks like this:

```
15    %let titltext=    B  o  o  k    S  a  l  e  s ;
16    %put WITHOUT Quoting Functions TITLTEXT=&titltext;
WITHOUT Quoting Functions TITLTEXT=B  o  o  k    S  a  l  e  s
17    %let titltext=%str(    B  o  o  k    S  a  l  e  s );
18    %put WITH Quoting Functions TITLTEXT=&titltext;
WITH Quoting Functions TITLTEXT=    B  o  o  k    S  a  l  e  s
```

Example: Using Quoting Functions to Mask Ampersands and Percent Signs

This example is for the ampersands (&) and percent signs (%).

```
%let reptext=Jan&Feb %Sales Report;
%put WITHOUT Quoting Functions REPTEXT=&reptext;
%let reptext=%nrstr(Jan&Feb %Sales Report);
%put WITH Quoting Functions REPTEXT=&reptext;
```

The SAS log for the previous statements looks like this:

```
WARNING: Apparent symbolic reference FEB not resolved.
WARNING: Apparent invocation of macro SALES not resolved.
19    %let reptext=Jan&Feb %Sales Report;
```

```
20    %put WITHOUT Quoting Functions REPTEXT=&reptext;
WARNING: Apparent symbolic reference FEB not resolved.
WARNING: Apparent invocation of macro SALES not resolved.
WITHOUT Quoting Functions REPTEXT=Jan&Feb %Sales Report
21    %let reptext=%nrstr(Jan&Feb %Sales Report);
22    %put WITH Quoting Functions REPTEXT=&reptext;
WITH Quoting Functions REPTEXT=Jan&Feb %Sales Report
```

Example: Using Quoting Functions to Mask Mnemonic Operators

This example is for treating mnemonic operators as text rather than using them as operators in a macro expression.

```
%let state=OR;
%let value=%sysevalf(&state eq OR, boolean);
%put WITHOUT Quoting Functions VALUE=&value;
%let value=%sysevalf( %bquote(&state) eq %bquote(OR), boolean);
%put WITH Quoting Functions VALUE=&value;
```

The SAS log for the previous statements looks like this:

```
23    %let state=OR;
24    %let value=%sysevalf(&state eq OR, boolean);
ERROR: A character operand was found in the %EVAL function or
%IF condition where a numeric operand is required. The
condition was: OR eq OR
25    %put WITHOUT Quoting Functions VALUE=&value;
WITHOUT Quoting Functions VALUE=
26    %let value=%sysevalf( %bquote(&state) eq %bquote(OR),
boolean);
27    %put WITH Quoting Functions VALUE=&value;
WITH Quoting Functions VALUE=1
```

Example: Using Macro Quoting Functions to Work with Unbalanced Quotation Marks

Last in this section is an example of working with unbalanced quotation marks. If you try the first four statements without a macro quoting function, the statements following these four statements will not execute properly.

Note that the %QSCAN macro function is used instead of the %SCAN macro function. The %QSCAN function quotes the result of the %SCAN function. The result contains an unmatched single quotation mark. If %SCAN was used, this unmatched single quotation mark would likely result in errors in the statements that follow. Therefore, %QSCAN is used to mask the single quotation mark in NAME3.

```
%let names=O'DONOVAN,O'HARA,O'MALLEY;
%let name3=%qscan(&names),3;
%put WITHOUT BQUOTE Quoting Function NAMES=&names;
%put WITHOUT BQUOTE Quoting Function NAME3=&name3;

%let names=%bquote(O'DONOVAN,O'HARA,O'MALLEY);
%let name3=%qscan(&names,3);
%put WITH BQUOTE Quoting Function NAMES=&names;
%put WITH BQUOTE Quoting Function NAME3=&name3;
```

Because of the errors generated with the first group of statements, only the SAS log for the second group is shown.

```
28    %let names=%bquote(O'DONOVAN,O'HARA,O'MALLEY);
29    %let name3=%qscan(&names,3);
30    %put WITH BQUOTE Quoting Function NAMES=&names;
WITH BQUOTE Quoting Function NAMES=O'DONOVAN,O'HARA,O'MALLEY
31    %put WITH BQUOTE Quoting Function NAME3=&name3;
WITH BQUOTE Quoting Function NAME3=O'MALLEY
```

Masking Special Characters and Mnemonic Operators at Macro Compilation

Sometimes your macro variable values will contain special characters or mnemonic operators and you do not want these items to be interpreted as macro triggers or operators. To prevent interpretation of these characters and operators at macro compilation, use the %STR and %NRSTR functions. Arguments to %STR and %NRSTR are treated as text. Further, at execution, these special characters and operators continue to be treated as text.

The %STR function masks all the characters and operators in Table 6.8 except for ampersands, percent signs, and unbalanced quotation marks and operators. The %NRSTR function does what the %STR function does, and also masks ampersands and percent signs.

When unmatched quotation marks or parentheses are used with %STR and %NRSTR, a percent sign must precede the unmatched character.

Several examples of %STR and %NRSTR are shown above.

Example: Using the %NRSTR Macro Function to Mask Special Characters and Mnemonic Operators at Compilation

In this example, the value of the NAMES macro variable contains ampersands. The %NRSTR function masks the ampersands in NAMES to prevent their interpretation as macro triggers or operators.

The macro variable NAMES also contains unmatched single quotation marks. Note that a percent sign precedes each unmatched single quotation mark.

```
%let names=%nrstr(O%'DONOVAN&O%'HARA&O%'MALLEY);
%let name3=%bquote(%scan( %bquote(&names),3));
%put &names;
%put NAME 3 is: &name3;
```

The SAS log of the preceding code follows.

```
32    %let names=%nrstr(O%'DONOVAN&O%'HARA&O%'MALLEY);
33    %let name3=%bquote(%scan( %bquote(&names),3));
34    %put &names;
O'DONOVAN&O'HARA&O'MALLEY
35    %put NAME 3 is: &name3;
NAME 3 is: O'MALLEY
```

Masking Special Characters and Mnemonic Operators at Execution

When the resolution of a macro expression contains special characters or mnemonic operators and you want the macro processor to ignore them, mask them with the %BQUOTE or the %NRBQUOTE macro functions. These two macro functions operate at execution after a macro expression has been resolved.

The %BQUOTE function masks all the characters and operators in Table 6.8 except for ampersands and percent signs. The %NRBQUOTE function does what the %BQUOTE function does, and also masks ampersands and percent signs.

These functions are commonly used with the %EVAL and %SYSEVALF functions. They are used with implicit references to the %EVAL function as well. Implicit references to %EVAL occur with macro language statements like %DO and %IF.

Examples of %BQUOTE and %NRBQUOTE are shown in the previous examples.

Masking Special Characters and Mnemonic Operators in a Macro Variable Value at Execution

The %SUPERQ function works at the time of macro execution to mask special characters and mnemonic operators that are in the value of a macro variable. This prevents resolution of the contents of a macro variable's value.

The argument to the %SUPERQ function is the name of the macro variable whose value is to be masked. The macro variable name is specified without a preceding ampersand.

The %SUPERQ function masks all the characters and operators in Table 6.8.

The %SUPERQ function operates similarly to the %NRBQUOTE function, but is more complete in its masking. With %NRBQUOTE, macro variable references and values are resolved before the argument is masked. With %SUPERQ, the masking is done before any macro variable references or values are resolved.

Example: Using the %SUPERQ Macro Function to Prevent Resolution of Special Characters in a Macro Variable

Following is an example of using %SUPERQ to mask the ampersands in a text string. The ampersands in the text argument are used as delimiters for the %SCAN function.

```
%let months=
   %nrstr(Jan&Feb&Mar&Apr&May&Jun&Jul&Aug&Sep&Oct&Nov&Dec);
%let month6=%scan( %superq(months),6);
%put &month6;
```

The SAS log for the above code is as follows:

```
36    %let months=
37       %nrstr(Jan&Feb&Mar&Apr&May&Jun&Jul&Aug&Sep&Oct&Nov&Dec);
38    %let month6=%scan( %superq(months),6);
39    %put &month6;
Jun
```

Unmasking Text and the %UNQUOTE Function

Occasionally you may need to restore the meaning of special characters and mnemonic operators that have been masked. The %UNQUOTE function communicates to the macro processor that you want the special characters and mnemonic operators resolved.

Example: Using the %UNQUOTE Macro Function to Cause Interpretation of a Masked Character

In the next example, the call to the macro program MAR has been masked and assigned to the macro variable XX. This text is placed in the first TITLE statement. To have the value of XX interpreted, the %UNQUOTE function must be used. The second TITLE statement contains the results of applying %UNQUOTE to the value of XX.

```
%macro mar;
   This is March
%mend;

%let xx=%nrstr(%mar);
title "Macro call &xx generates the following text";
```

```
title2 "%unquote(&xx)";
```

The TITLE statements after submission of the above code are as follows:

```
          Macro call %mar generates the following text
                     This is March
```

Using Other Quoting Functions

The results of macro character functions are unmasked or unquoted. Special characters and mnemonic operators in the results are resolved. If you want to mask the special characters or mnemonic operators in a result, use the "quoting" version of the macro character function.

The quoting versions of macro character functions are listed in Table 6.1 following their "unquoted" counterparts. An example of %QSCAN was shown earlier in this chapter. Another example of a quoting version of a macro character function follows.

Example: Using the %QSUBSTR Macro Function to Mask the Results of the %SUBSTR Macro Function

This next example uses the %QSUBSTR macro function to mask the results of the %SUBSTR macro function.

The macro variable MONTH3 is defined by using the %SUBSTR macro function. This action results in warning messages because the macro processor tries to resolve the ampersand in the result of the %SUBSTR function.

The macro variable QMONTH3 is defined by using the %QSUBSTR macro function. The %QSUBSTR macro function masks the ampersand in the extraction. No warning messages are generated because the macro processor ignores the ampersand in the result of the %QSUBSTR macro function.

```
%let months=%nrstr(Jan&Feb&Mar);
%let month3=%substr(&months,8);
%put Unquoted: &month3;

%let qmonth3=%qsubstr(&months,8);
%put Quoted: &qmonth3;
```

The SAS log for the above code follows. Note that the warnings correspond to macro variable MONTH3 and the unquoted result of the substring function.

```
40    %let months=%nrstr(Jan&Feb&Mar);
41    %let month3=%substr(&months,8);
WARNING: Apparent symbolic reference MAR not resolved.
42    %put Unquoted: &month3;
WARNING: Apparent symbolic reference MAR not resolved.
Unquoted: &Mar
43
44    %let qmonth3=%qsubstr(&months,8);
45    %put Quoted: &qmonth3;

Quoted: &Mar
```

CHAPTER 7

Interfaces to the Macro Facility

The interfaces described in this chapter provide you with a dynamic link for communication between the SAS language and the macro facility. Until now, the discussion of the macro facility has emphasized the distinction between when macro language statements are resolved and when SAS language statements are resolved. With these interfaces, your SAS language programs can direct the actions of the macro processor.

The interfaces described in this chapter include

- SAS language functions and routines

- PROC SQL

- SAS Component Language functions and routines

- SAS/CONNECT.

DATA Step Interfaces

Two functions and two routines in the SAS language can interact with the macro processor *during* execution of the DATA step. These four tools are listed in Table 7.1.

Table 7.1   DATA Step interface tools

Tool	Description
SYMGET(*argument*)	SAS language function that obtains a macro variable value during DATA step execution.
CALL SYMPUT(*macro-variable, value*);	SAS language routine that assigns *value* produced in a DATA step to a *macro-variable*.
CALL EXECUTE(*argument*);	SAS language routine that executes the resolved value of *argument*. Arguments that resolve to a macro facility reference execute immediately. Any SAS language statements resulting from the resolution are executed at the end of the step.
RESOLVE(*argument*)	SAS language function that resolves *argument* during DATA step execution. Text expressions include macro variables and macro program calls.

The SYMGET Function

The SYMGET SAS language function retrieves macro variable values from the macro symbol tables during execution of a data step. Data set variables can then be created and updated with information that is retrieved from the macro processor.

The syntax of the SYMGET function is

```
SYMGET(argument)
```

The SYMGET function accepts three types of arguments:

- the name of a macro variable that is enclosed in single quotation marks and without the leading ampersand. In the following example, X is a macro variable that was defined earlier in the program.

```
y=symget('x');
```

- the name of a DATA step character variable whose value is the name of a macro variable.

```
%let webdesig=1.33;
data temp;
   set ....;
```

```
attrib costsect length=$8 label='Section';
*----When section=Web Design, costsect="WEBDESIG";
costsect=substr(compress(section),1,8);
costfctr=symget(costsect);
....
```

- a DATA step character expression. The resolution of the character expression is the name of a macro variable.

```
%let fctr1997=1.30;
%let fctr1998=1.27;
%let fctr1999=1.10;
data calcs;
   set totals;
   array totl{3} totl1997-totl1999;
   do year=1997 to 1999;
     totl{year-1996}=symget('fctr' || put(year,4.)) *
                     totl{year-1996};
   end;
run;
```

The value that SYMGET retrieves is always a character value. By default, the DATA step variable that SYMGET creates is a character variable with a length of 200 bytes. The DATA step variable can be defined with a shorter length using the LENGTH or ATTRIB statement. If the DATA step variable has been defined as numeric, the SAS System attempts to convert the value that SYMGET retrieves to a number and writes a warning message to the SAS log.

More examples of the three types of arguments that SYMGET can receive follow.

Example: Using the SYMGET Function by Directly Naming the Macro Variables

In the first program, the values of two macro variables are transferred to specific observations in the data set.

```
%let webfctr=1.20;
%let intfctr=1.35;

data temp;
   set books.ytdsales(where=(
      section in ('Web Design', 'Internet'));
   if section='Web Design' then costfctr=symget('webfctr');
   else if section='Internet' then costfctr=symget('intfctr');
   newprice=costfctr*cost;
run;
```

```
proc print data=temp;
  title "Prices based on COSTFCTR";
  var section cost costfctr newpric;
  format newpric dollar8.2;
run;
```

A partial listing of the PROC PRINT (Figure 7.1) shows that the COSTFCTR variable was created for each observation in the data set. The value of COSTFCTR depends on the value of SECTION.

Figure 7.1   Partial output from direct reference to macro variable in SYMGET

```
                    Prices based on COSTFCTR                          1

        OBS     SECTION          COST     COSTFCTR     NEWPRICE

          1     Internet        $20.97      1.35        $28.30
          2     Internet        $23.07      1.35        $31.14
          3     Internet        $23.07      1.35        $31.14
          4     Internet        $17.47      1.35        $23.58
          5     Internet        $25.17      1.35        $33.97
  . . .
       1778     Web Design      $25.17      1.20        $30.20
       1779     Web Design      $23.07      1.20        $27.68
       1780     Web Design      $20.27      1.20        $24.32
       1781     Web Design      $20.97      1.20        $25.16
       1782     Web Design      $23.07      1.20        $27.68
       1783     Web Design      $13.27      1.20        $15.92
```

Example: Using a Data Set Variable Name as the Argument to the SYMGET Function

The next example shows how the value of a data set variable can be used to look up a macro variable value. The data set variable COSTSECT holds the name of the macro variable containing the cost factor value for the observation. COSTSECT equals the first eight characters of the section name.

```
%let internet=1.25;
%let networks=1.20;
%let operatin=1.30;
%let programm=1.28;
%let webdesig=1.33;

data temp;
  set books.ytdsales;
  costsect=substr(compress(section),1,8);
  costfctr=symget(costsect);
  newprice=cost*costfctr;
run;
```

```
proc print data=temp;
  title "Prices based on COSTFCTR";
  var section costsect cost costfctr newprice;
  format newprice dollar8.2;
run;
```

A partial listing of the PROC PRINT (Figure 7.2) shows that the COSTFCTR variable was created for each observation in the data set. The value of COSTFCTR depends on the value of SECTION.

Figure 7.2   Partial output from using a data set variable as an argument to SYMGET

```
                    Prices based on COSTFCTR                          1

  OBS     SECTION       COSTSECT         COST     COSTFCTR     NEWPRICE

    1     Internet      Internet        $20.97      1.25        $26.21
    2     Internet      Internet        $23.07      1.25        $28.83
    3     Internet      Internet        $23.07      1.25        $28.83
  . . .
 1778     Networks  and Communication
                        Networks        $20.27      1.20        $24.32
 1779     Networks  and Communication
                        Networks        $27.97      1.20        $33.56
 1780     Networks  and Communication
                        Networks        $23.07      1.20        $27.68
  . . .
 2427     Operating Systems
                        Operatin        $17.47      1.30        $22.70
 2428     Operating Systems
                        Operatin        $20.27      1.30        $26.34
 2429     Operating Systems
                        Operatin        $17.47      1.30        $22.70
  . . .
 4304     Programming Languages
                        Programm        $17.47      1.28        $22.36
 4305     Programming Languages
                        Programm        $20.27      1.28        $25.94
 4306     Programming Languages
                        Programm        $23.07      1.28        $29.52
  . . .
 5204     Web Design    WebDesig        $25.17      1.33        $33.47
 5205     Web Design    WebDesig        $23.07      1.33        $30.68
 5206     Web Design    WebDesig        $20.27      1.33        $26.95
```

Example: Using the Result of Resolving a Character Expression as an Argument to the SYMGET Function

The next program resolves SAS language character expressions to obtain the names and values of macro variables. Four macro variables are created. Each macro variable holds an adjustment factor for a year. PROC MEANS calculates total sales per section in the bookstore. A DATA step multiplies the section factors stored in the macro variables by the total sales value. PROC PRINT displays the data set.

```
%let adj1997=1.10;
%let adj1998=1.15;
%let adj1999=1.18;
%let adj2000=1.05;

proc means data=books.ytdsales sum noprint nway;
   class section;
   var salepric;
   output out=sumsales sum=salepric;
run;

data temp;
   set sumsales;
   array adj{4} adj1997-adj2000;
   array sale{4} sale1997-sale2000;
   do year=1997 to 2000;
      idx=year-1996;
      adj{idx}=symget('adj' || put(year,4.));
      sale{idx}=salepric*adj{idx};
   end;
run;

proc print data=temp;
   title 'Adjusted Sales';
   var section salepric adj1997 sale1997 adj1998 sale1998
                        adj1999 sale1999 adj2000 sale2000;
   format sale1997-sale2000 dollar10.2;
run;
```

The PROC PRINT output for this program is in Figure 7.3.

Figure 7.3   Output from resolving character expressions as arguments to the SYMGET function

```
                             Adjusted Sales                               1

    OBS  SECTION                          SALEPRIC   ADJ1997      SALE1997

     1   Internet                        $53998.95    1.1       $59,398.84
     2   Networks and Communication      $19472.97    1.1       $21,420.26
     3   Operating Systems               $56964.04    1.1       $62,660.45
     4   Programming Languages           $26830.81    1.1       $29,513.89
     5   Web Design                      $53321.45    1.1       $58,653.60

    OBS  ADJ1998     SALE1998 ADJ1999    SALE1999 ADJ2000      SALE2000

     1    1.15    $62,098.79    1.18   $63,718.76   1.05   $56,698.90
     2    1.15    $22,393.91    1.18   $22,978.10   1.05   $20,446.61
     3    1.15    $65,508.65    1.18   $67,217.57   1.05   $59,812.25
     4    1.15    $30,855.43    1.18   $31,660.36   1.05   $28,172.35
     5    1.15    $61,319.67    1.18   $62,919.32   1.05   $55,987.53
```

The SYMPUT Routine

The SYMPUT SAS language routine creates macro variables during execution of a DATA step. If the macro variable already exists, CALL SYMPUT updates the macro variable value.

The syntax of the SYMPUT routine is:

```
CALL SYMPUT(macro-variable,text)
```

The two arguments to CALL SYMPUT can each be specified in one of the following three ways.

- literal text. The following SAS language statement creates or updates the macro variable BOOKSECT with the value *Internet*. CALL SYMPUT is a SAS language routine. Therefore, literal text arguments are enclosed in single quotation marks.

```
call symput('booksect','Internet');
```

- the name of a data set variable. The current value of the data set variable NHIGH is assigned to the macro variable N35.

```
call symput('N35',nhigh);
```

- a DATA step expression. The result of evaluating the expression is assigned to the macro variable SALES.

```
call symput('sales',trim(left(section)) || ' ' ||
                 put(totsales,dollar10.2));
```

CALL SYMPUT updates the value of a macro variable. A macro variable can only have one value. Although CALL SYMPUT can be executed with each pass of the DATA step, it will still have only one value. An illustration of this concept follows.

Example: Executing CALL SYMPUT Once in a DATA Step

In the next program, CALL SYMPUT creates a macro variable that contains the total number of books that sold for more than $35.00 each. CALL SYMPUT is executed once when the DATA step reaches the end of the data set.

If CALL SYMPUT was executed for each observation in the data set, the macro variable value would be updated with each observation. Since we only want the final value, we only need to execute CALL SYMPUT once and that is done when the DATA step reaches the end-of-file.

```
data temp;
   set books.ytdsales end=eof;
   if salepric ge 35 then nhigh+1;
   if eof then call symput('n35',nhigh);
run;
```

Example: Executing CALL SYMPUT Multiple Times in a DATA Step

In the next program, CALL SYMPUT is executed for each observation in the data set. The value of the macro variable at the end of the DATA step is the value from the last observation in the data set.

```
data books;
   input title $ 1-40;
   call symput('booktitl',trim(title));
cards;
Wonderful Web Pages
Easy Networks
Jiffy Java
Web Sites of the Rich and Famous
;
```

```
%put The value of macro variable BOOKTITL is &booktitl..;
```

The %PUT statement writes the following to the SAS log.

```
The value of macro variable BOOKTITL is Web Sites of the Rich
and Famous.
```

Example: Creating Several Macro Variables with CALL SYMPUT

The next example shows how to create multiple macro variables with CALL SYMPUT. This program creates two macro variables for each section in the output data set produced by PROC FREQ. There are five sections in the output data set. Therefore, ten macro variables are created. Five macro variables hold the names of the five sections. The other five macro variables hold the frequency counts for each of the sections. A %PUT _USER_ lists the ten macro variables created in the DATA step.

```
proc freq data=books.ytdsales noprint;
   tables section / out=sectname;
run;
data _null_;
  set sectname;
  call symput('name' || put(_n_,1.),section);
  call symput('n' || put(_n_,1.),count);
run;

%put _user_;
```

The %PUT _USER_ writes the following to the SAS log:

```
GLOBAL NAME1 Internet
GLOBAL N1        1777
GLOBAL NAME2 Networks and Communication
GLOBAL N2         649
GLOBAL NAME3 Operating Systems
GLOBAL N3        1877
GLOBAL NAME4 Programming Languages
GLOBAL N4         900
GLOBAL NAME5 Web Design
GLOBAL N5        1756
```

Understanding the Timing of CALL SYMPUT

The macro variable that CALL SYMPUT creates cannot be successfully referenced until the DATA step containing CALL SYMPUT finishes. As described earlier, macro variable references are resolved by the macro processor at compilation. However, macro variables created by CALL SYMPUT do not *exist* until *execution* of CALL SYMPUT in the DATA step. Therefore, at compilation, a reference to a macro variable created by CALL SYMPUT within that DATA step cannot be resolved because the macro variable does not yet exist.

The following program creates a macro variable with CALL SYMPUT. The macro variable is referenced in the same DATA step by assigning its value to a data set variable. The SAS language PUT statement demonstrates that this assignment does not occur. The %PUT statement demonstrates that the macro variable has a value after the DATA step finishes. A PROC PRINT of the data set further shows that the value was not assigned to the data set variable Y.

```
data temp;
   call symput('x','Web Design');
   y="&x";
   put y=;
run;

%put Macro variable X created by SYMPUT equals &x..;

proc print data=temp;
   title "Data set TEMP";
   title2 "Data set variable Y could not be updated with the";
   title3 "value of macro variable X";
run;
```

The SAS log of this program follows.

```
1      data temp;
2         call symput('x','Web Design');
3            y="&x";
WARNING: Apparent symbolic reference X not resolved.
4         put Data Set Variable y=;
5      run;

Data Set Variable Y=&x
NOTE: The data set WORK.TEMP has 1 observations and 1
variables.
NOTE: The DATA statement used 0.39 seconds.

6
7    %put Macro variable X created by SYMPUT equals &x..;
Macro variable X created by SYMPUT equals Web Design.
8
9    proc print data=temp;
10      title "Data set TEMP";
11      title2 "Data set variable Y could not be updated with
the";
12      title3 "value of macro variable X";
13   run;

NOTE: The PROCEDURE PRINT used 0.33 seconds
```

The output for the PROC PRINT step in is Figure 7.4.

Figure 7.4   Output for PROC PRINT of data set that could not be updated with the macro variable value

```
                               Data set TEMP                              1
               Data set variable Y could not be updated with the
                         value of macro variable X

                               OBS     Y

                                1      &x
```

The next DATA step and PROC step are submitted just after the one above. This time the macro variable X is successfully resolved because at the time of execution of this DATA step, the macro variable X exists.

```
data temp2;
   y="&x";
run;
proc print data=temp2;
   title "Data set TEMP2";
   title2 "Macro Variable X now exists, so Y can be updated";
   title3 "with the value of macro variable X";
run;
```

The SAS log for the two steps follows.

```
14    data temp2;
15       y="&x";
16    run;

NOTE: The data set WORK.TEMP2 has 1 observations and 1
variables.
NOTE: The DATA statement used 0.11 seconds.

17    proc print data=temp2;
18       title "Data set TEMP2";
19       title2 "Macro Variable X now exists, so Y can be
updated";
20       title3 "with the value of macro variable X";
21    run;

NOTE: The PROCEDURE PRINT used 0.05 seconds.
```

The output for the PROC PRINT step is in Figure 7.5.

Figure 7.5   **Output for PROC PRINT of data set that could be updated with the macro variable value**

```
                      Data set TEMP2                    2
        Macro Variable X now exists, so Y can be updated
               with the value of macro variable X


                    OBS          Y

                     1        Web Design
```

The CALL EXECUTE Routine

The CALL EXECUTE SAS language routine allows you to specify execution of macro programs and resolution of macro variable references from the DATA step. With CALL EXECUTE, you can write SAS language statements to conditionally execute macro programs from within DATA steps.

The CALL EXECUTE routine generates calls to the macro processor during execution of the DATA step. Calls to the macro processor made by CALL EXECUTE execute immediately when encountered during execution of the DATA step. However, if the arguments to CALL EXECUTE resolve to SAS language statements, these statements execute after the DATA step finishes.

The syntax of the CALL EXECUTE routine is

```
call execute('argument')
```

The three types of arguments that can be supplied to the routine are:

- a text string enclosed in quotation marks. Single quotation marks and double quotation marks are handled differently. Single quotation marks cause the argument to be resolved when the DATA step executes. Double quotation marks cause the argument to be resolved by the macro processor during construction of the DATA step, before compilation and execution.

- the name of a data set character variable. The value of this variable can be a text expression or a SAS language statement. This variable name should not be enclosed in quotation marks.

- a text expression that is resolved by the DATA step to a SAS language statement or to a macro variable, macro statement, or macro program reference.

Example: Using CALL EXECUTE to Conditionally Call a Macro Program

The next program uses CALL EXECUTE to conditionally execute a macro program. First, PROC MEANS computes the sales for each section and stores them in a data set. When the sales are over $10,000, CALL EXECUTE calls the macro program REPHIGH.

The argument to CALL EXECUTE is the macro program name. The one parameter to the macro program is the section name. The section name is added to the CALL EXECUTE expression.

The SAS language statements in the macro program execute when the DATA step finishes. In this example, the CALL EXECUTE routine executes as many times as there are observations that satisfy the IF statement condition. Each time CALL EXECUTE executes, the macro program REPHIGH is called. Therefore, when the DATA step finishes, there may be several PROC REPORT steps ready to process.

```
%macro rephigh(section);
   proc report data=books.ytdsales headline center nowindows;
     where section="&section";
     column  ( title n salepric );
     define  title / group spacing=2   left "Title of Book" ;
     define  n / width=6   spacing=2   right "n" ;
     define  salepric / sum format= dollar9.2 width=9 spacing=2
     right "Sale Price" ;
   run;
%mend;

proc means data=books.ytdsales;
   class section;
   var salepric;
   output out=sectsale sum=totlsale;
run;

data _null_;
   set sectsale;

   if totlsale > 10000 then
     call execute('%rephigh(' || section || ')');
run;
```

Example: Using CALL EXECUTE to Select Which Macro Program to Call

The next example shows how you can conditionally call different macro programs during the execution of a DATA step. The SAS language statements that result from the macro program calls are executed after the DATA step ends. When sales for a section are below $5,000, LOWREPT is

called. When sales are above $10,000, HIGHREPT is called. The value of the data set variable
SECTION is passed as a parameter to each of the macro programs.

```
%macro highrept(Section);
    title "Section &section with sales > $10000";
    proc means data=books.ytdsales n sum;
      class saleinit;
      where section="&section";
      var salepric;
    run;
%mend;

%macro lowrept(section);
    title "Section &section with sales < $5000";
    proc print data=books.ytdsales;
      where section="&section";
      var title salepric;
    run;
%mend;

proc means data=books.ytdsales noprint sum nway;
  class section;
  var salepric;
  output out=sectsale sum=totlsect;
run;

data _null_;
  set sectsale;
  if totlsect < 5000 then
    call execute('%lowrept(' || section || ')');
  else if totlsect > 10000 then
    call execute('%highrept(' || section || ')');
run;
```

The RESOLVE Function

The RESOLVE function resolves a reference to the macro facility during execution of a DATA
step. The result is assigned to a SAS data set variable in the DATA step. The RESOLVE function
is a SAS language function and belongs in the DATA step in SAS language statements.

The syntax of the RESOLVE function is

```
resolve('argument')
```

The three types of arguments that RESOLVE accepts are:

• a text expression that is enclosed in single quotation marks. This text expression is a macro
  variable reference, an open code macro language statement, or a macro program call. If the
  text expression was enclosed in double quotation marks, the macro processor would try to

resolve it before compilation and execution, while the SAS program is being constructed. Enclosing the argument in single quotation marks delays resolution until execution of the DATA step.

```
dsvar=resolve('&macvar');
```

- the name of a data set character variable. The value of this variable is a text expression representing a macro variable reference, an open code macro language statement, or a macro program call.

```
%let lbl1=All the Books Sold;
data temp;
   length txtlabel $ 40;
   macexp='&lbl1';
   txtlabel=resolve(macexp);
run;
```

- a character expression that can be resolved to a text expression. The text expression represents a macro variable reference, an open code macro language statement, or a macro program call.

```
%let sect1=Sales for Internet;
%let sect2=Sales for Web Design;
data temp;
   set summsale(obs=2);
   length sectname $ 40;
   sectlbl=resolve('&sect' || put(_n_,1.));
run;
```

The length of the text value returned by RESOLVE is the maximum length of a DATA step character variable. If you want the character variable to be shorter than the maximum, you must explicitly define a shorter length for the variable. This can be done with the LENGTH statement or with the ATTRIB statement.

The RESOLVE function is more versatile than the SYMGET function: RESOLVE resolves any macro expression while SYMGET only resolves references to macro variables.

With RESOLVE, you can obtain the value of a macro variable created by CALL SYMPUT in the same DATA step in which it was created.

Example: Using the RESOLVE Function to Obtain a Macro Variable Value for Use in the Same DATA Step

The following example shows how RESOLVE can be used with CALL SYMPUT in the same DATA step. This program is a modified version of one of the programs in the section on CALL SYMPUT.

```
data temp;
   length section $ 40;
   call symput('sectmvar','Web Design');
   section=resolve('&sectmvar');
   put section=;
run;

proc print data=temp;
   title 'Data Set TEMP';
   title2 'Macro variable SECTMVAR can be referenced in';
   title3 'the same DATA step it was created with RESOLVE';
run;
```

The SAS log of the SAS language PUT statement in the DATA step shows that the data set variable was updated with the value of the macro variable SECTMVAR.

```
19    data temp;
20       length section $ 40;
21       call symput('sectmvar','Web Design');
22       section=resolve('&sectmvar');
23       put section=;
24    run;

SECTION=Web Design
```

A PROC PRINT of the data set also shows that the data set variable SECTION was updated with the value of macro variable SECTMVAR (Figure 7.6).

Figure 7.6   PROC PRINT of the data set containing a variable updated with the RESOLVE function

```
                        Data Set TEMP                        1
             Macro variable SECTMVAR can be referenced in
           the same DATA step it was created with RESOLVE

                        OBS      SECTION

                         1      Web Design
```

PROC SQL and the Macro Facility

If you use PROC SQL, you can use the macro facility in your PROC SQL steps. PROC SQL steps can create and update macro variables during execution of PROC SQL. PROC SQL also creates and maintains three macro variables that hold information about the processing of a PROC SQL step.

This section describes only the macro facility interface features of PROC SQL. For complete information on PROC SQL, refer to PROC SQL documentation.

Creating and Updating Macro Variables with PROC SQL

The INTO clause on the SELECT statement creates and updates macro variables. Calculations that are done with the SELECT statement can be stored in macro variables specified on the INTO clause. Entire data columns can also be stored in the macro variables that are named on the INTO clause.

The INTO clause is analogous to the CALL SYMPUT routine in the DATA step. Like CALL SYMPUT, the INTO clause creates and updates macro variables during execution of the step. In the case of the INTO clause, the step is PROC SQL.

The INTO clause provides a link to the macro variable symbol table during execution of PROC SQL. Values that are assigned to the macro variables are considered to be text.

The macro variables that you create with PROC SQL are added to the most local macro symbol table available when PROC SQL executes. If PROC SQL is not submitted from within a macro program, the macro variables are stored in the global macro symbol table.

The basic syntax of the INTO clause on the PROC SQL SELECT statement follows:

```
SELECT col1,col2,...
       INTO :macvar1, :macvar2,...
       FROM table-expression
       WHERE where-expression
       other clauses;
```

Note the punctuation on the INTO clause: the macro variable names are preceded with colons (:), not ampersands (&). Macro variables are explicitly named on the INTO clause. Numbered lists of macro variables can also be specified on the INTO clause. Examples of both follow.

Leading and trailing blanks are removed from the values that are assigned to the macro variables unless the NOTRIM option follows the macro variable specification.

The INTO clause cannot be used during creation of a table or view. It may only be used on outer queries of the SELECT statement.

Example: Using the INTO Clause in PROC SQL to Create Macro Variables

A simple example of the INTO clause follows. Total sales and the total number of books sold are stored in two macro variables, TOTSALES and NSOLD. The %PUT statement following the step writes the values of these two global macro variables to the SAS log.

```
proc sql;
   select sum(salepric),count(salepric)
     into :totsales,:nsold
     from books.ytdsales;
quit;
%put &totsales &nsold;
```

Now try the above example without the SUM and COUNT functions. The macro variables TOTSALES and NSOLD now each equal the value of SALEPRIC in the first row of the table. The default action of the INTO statement is to store the first row of the table in the macro variables on the INTO clause.

Example: Using the INTO Clause in PROC SQL to Create a Macro Variable for Each Row in a Table

Numbered lists on the INTO clause can store rows of a table in macro variables. The next program stores the sales for the five computer sections in the five macro variables SALE1, SALE2, SALE3, SALE4, and SALE5. The five section names are stored in SECT1, SECT2, SECT3, SECT4, and SECT5.

```
proc sql;
   select section,sum(salepric)
     into :sect1 - :sect5, :sale1 - :sale5
     from books.ytdsales
     group by section;
quit;
%put &sect1 &sale1;
%put &sect2 &sale2;
%put &sect3 &sale3;
%put &sect4 &sale4;
%put &sect5 &sale5;
```

The SAS log of the above program follows:

```
229  %put &sect1 &sale1;
Internet 53998.95
230  %put &sect2 &sale2;
Networks and Communication 19472.97
231  %put &sect3 &sale3;
Operating Systems 56964.04
```

```
232  %put &sect4 &sale4;
Programming Languages 26830.81
233  %put &sect5 &sale5;
Web Design 53321.45
```

Example: Storing All Values of a Table Column in One Macro Variable

Another interesting feature of the INTO clause stores all values of a column in a macro variable. These values are stored side-by-side. To do this, add the SEPARATED BY feature to the INTO clause. The previous example is modified below so that all section names are stored in the macro variable ALLSECT.

```
proc sql;
   select unique(section)
   into :allsect separated by ','
   from books.ytdsales
   order by section;
quit;
%put &allsect;
```

The SAS log after execution of the above step follows:

```
310  %put &allsect;
Internet,Networks and Communication,Operating
Systems,Programming Languages,Web Design
```

Using the Macro Variables Created by PROC SQL

PROC SQL creates and updates three macro variables that you can make use of in your programs. These macro variables are created by the SAS System when you run PROC SQL and they are stored in the global macro symbol table. You can use the values of the macro variables in your macro programs to control execution of your SAS programs. The three PROC SQL macro variables are listed in Table 7.2.

Table 7.2   Macro variables created by PROC SQL

Macro Variable	Description
SQLOBS	set to the number of rows produced with a SELECT statement
SQLRC	set to the return code from an SQL statement
SQLOOPS	set to the number of iterations of the inner loop of PROC SQL

The Pass-Through facility of PROC SQL also creates two macro variables, SQLXRC and SQLXMSG. These macro variables contain information about error conditions that may have occurred in the processing of Pass-Through SQL statements. For complete information on these macro variables, refer to SAS/Access documentation. The two macro variables are described in Table 7.3.

Table 7.3   PROC SQL macro variables used with the Pass-Through facility

Macro Variable	Description
SQLXRC	set to the return code generated by a Pass-Through facility statement
SQLXMSG	set to descriptive information about the error generated by a Pass-Through SQL statement.

Example: Using the PROC SQL SQLOBS Automatic Macro Variables

The following example uses the SQLOBS automatic macro variable to define the number of macro variables needed in a SELECT statement. The first SELECT statement updates the SQLOBS macro variable. The second SELECT statement uses the SQLOBS macro variable to determine the total number of macro variables that the INTO clause should create. Each section name is stored in a macro variable. These section names are listed when the macro program LISTSECT is executed.

```
proc sql;
   select unique(section)
   from books.ytdsales
   order by section;
   select unique(section)
   into :sect1 - :sect&sqlobs
   from books.ytdsales
   order by section;
quit;

%macro listsect;
   %put Total number of sections: &sqlobs..;
   %do i=1 %to &sqlobs;
      %put Section &i: &&sect&i;
   %end;
%mend;

%listsect
```

The SAS log after LISTSECT executes follows:

```
Total number of sections: 5.
Section 1: Internet
Section 2: Networks and Communication
Section 3: Operating Systems
Section 4: Programming Languages
Section 5: Web Design
```

SAS Component Language and the Macro Facility

Macro facility features can be incorporated in your SAS Component Language (SCL) programs. SCL programs are compiled and executed the same way as SAS language programs. The word scanner tokenizes the SCL statements and passes the tokens on to the SCL compiler for compilation. Macro variables references in SCL programs outside of SUBMIT blocks are resolved during tokenization and compilation. SCL programs are executed when they are called.

Macro variable references and macro programs are processed in much the same way as they are in SAS language programs. However, many SCL features can accomplish the same tasks as the macro facility. Using SCL features instead of macro facility features may be preferable in order to make your SCL programs easier to follow and maintain.

This section describes the functions and routines that are used to access the macro facility from within your SCL programs. It also describes how you can use macro variables in your SCL SUBMIT blocks and how these macro variables relate to SCL variables.

Using the Macro Facility to Pass Information between SCL Programs

The macro facility can pass information between SCL programs. A global macro variable created in one SCL program can be referenced in another SCL program. The SYMGET function and the SYMPUT routine can pass macro variable values between SCL programs when the SCL programs execute. Otherwise, any other references to macro variables resolve at compilation of the SCL program.

The SYMGET function and the SYMPUT routine operate the same in SCL as they do in the SAS language DATA step. In SCL, these tools update and retrieve information from the global macro symbol table during execution of the SCL program. Refer to the sections above on SYMGET and SYMPUT for more information on these tools.

In addition, SCL has the SYMGETN function and the SYMPUTN routine. The SYMGETN function returns the value of the global macro variable as a numeric value. The SYMPUTN function assigns a numeric value to a global macro variable.

Even though the macro facility can pass information between SCL programs, it may be easier to follow and maintain your programs if you use the SCL CALL statement with parameters and the associated ENTRY statement in the called program.

Example: Creating a Macro Variable in an SCL Program

The following example shows part of an SCL program that processes the initials that the user enters and then creates a macro variable containing those initials.

```
array okinits{*} $ 3 ('MJM' 'JMB' 'BLT');

init:
  control label;
return;

term:
return;

inits:
  erroroff inits;
  if inits not in okinits then do;
    erroron inits;
    _msg_='NOTE: Please enter valid initials.';
  end;
  else do;
    call symput('USERINIT',inits);
  end;
return;
```

The next program excerpt executes after the previous program. This program obtains the user's initials at the time of execution by using the SYMGET function.

```
length inits $ 3;

init:
  inits=symget('USERINIT');
return;

main:
  .
  .
  .
```

Referencing Macro Variables in SUBMIT Blocks

Macro variable references in SCL programs are resolved at the time of tokenization and compilation. The exception to this is when SAS programs in SUBMIT blocks contain macro variable references.

Macro variable references in SUBMIT blocks do not resolve until the SAS program in the SUBMIT block is tokenized. During tokenization, the SAS System first checks to see if the macro variable reference corresponds to an SCL variable in the SCL program. If it does, the value of the

SCL variable is substituted for the reference in the SAS program. If it does not, the macro processor then takes over and looks for the macro variable in the global symbol table.

To force the resolution of a macro variable reference by the macro processor and skip resolution by the SCL program, precede the macro variable reference with two ampersands.

Example: Using SUBMIT Blocks that Contain Macro Variables

The following example shows two SUBMIT blocks for two SAS programs that each reference a macro variable. Assume that there is a field on the SCL program screen for the user to enter a report date. When the user leaves this field blank and selects to run a report, the program in the first SUBMIT block executes. When the user specifies a report date, the program in the second SUBMIT block executes.

Both SUBMIT blocks reference a macro variable with the same name as the SCL variable. In the first SUBMIT block, two ampersands precede the macro variable name. Only the macro processor attempts to resolve the reference. In the second SUBMIT block, one ampersand precedes the macro variable name. Therefore, the SCL program is first to attempt resolution of the reference.

```
init:
  control label;
  repdate=_blank_;
return;

term:
return;

runrep:
  if repdate=_blank_ then link reptoday;
  else link specrep;
  repdate=_blank_;
return;

reptoday:
  _msg_='NOTE: Today''s report is processing....';
  submit continue;
    %let repdate=&sysdate;
    proc print data=books.ytdsales;
      where saledate="&&repdate"D;
      title "Report for &&repdate";
      var section title salepric;
    run;
  endsubmit;
return;

specrep:
  _msg_='NOTE: Past date report is processing....';
  submit continue;
```

```
   proc means data=books.ytdsales n sum;
     title "Sales Report for past date: &repdate";
     where saledate="&repdate"D;
     class section;
     var salepric;
   run;
 endsubmit;
return;
```

SAS/CONNECT and the Macro Facility

The %SYSRPUT macro language statement is used with SAS/CONNECT to retrieve the value of a macro variable stored on a remote host. The %SYSRPUT statement is processed on the remote host. The value that is retrieved by %SYSRPUT is then stored in a macro variable in the local SAS session. The %SYSRPUT statement can be submitted from open code or from within a macro program.

The syntax of %SYSRPUT is as follows:

```
%SYSRPUT local-macro-variable=remote-macro-variable;
```

User-defined local macro variable names and remote macro variable names are not preceded with ampersands on the %SYSRPUT statement. Global automatic macro variable names are preceded with ampersands.

The %SYSRPUT statement is especially useful for obtaining system information from the remote host and making it available to your local session.

Example: Using %SYSRPUT to Obtain an Automatic Macro Variable Value from a Remote Host

The following example uses %SYSRPUT to obtain the value of the automatic macro variable SYSINFO on the remote host. SYSINFO holds return codes that are generated at the completion of SAS procedures. This use of %SYSRPUT checks to see if the PROC MEANS step executed without errors on the remote host. When the PROC MEANS step successfully processes, the PROC PRINT step is run locally. When the PROC MEANS does not execute, a message is written to the SAS log of the local session.

This SAS program is submitted to a remote MVS/TSO host with the RSUBMIT command.

```
%macro dohost;
  libname remote 'books.allstors.sasdata' disp=shr;
  libname local 'c:\books';
  proc means data=remote.masterds noprint;
    class section store;
    var salepric;
    output out=local.storsale n=nsold sum=sumsales;
  run;

  %sysrput rc=&sysinfo;

  %if &rc=0 %then %do;
    proc print data=local.storsale;
      title 'Data Set Summarized by Host and Stored Locally';
    run;
  %end;
  %else %do;
    %put Data set was not summarized and stored locally.;
  %end;
%mend;


%dohost
```

CHAPTER 8

Storing and Reusing Macro Programs

As your macro programming skills develop, you will find uses for your macro programs in several different applications. You may want to share these macro programs with your co-workers and make these macro programs available to your batch jobs. Since reusability is one of the great features of macro programs, it makes sense that there would be a systematic way to store macro programs in the SAS System. In fact, there are two ways to store your macro programs in the SAS System: the autocall facility and the stored compiled macro facility.

The autocall facility consists of external files or SOURCE entries in SAS catalogs that contain your macro programs. When you specify certain SAS options, the macro processor searches your autocall libraries when it is resolving a macro program reference.

The stored compiled macro facility consists of SAS catalogs that contain compiled macro programs. When you specify certain SAS options, the macro processor searches your catalogs of compiled macro programs when it is resolving a macro program reference.

This chapter describes how to use these two tools. It also briefly addresses host system issues related to these tools.

Saving Macro Programs with the Autocall Facility

When you store a macro program in an autocall library, you do not have to submit the macro program for compilation before you reference the macro program. The macro processor does that for you if it finds the macro program in the autocall library.

Several SAS products ship with libraries of macro programs that you can reference, or that are referenced by the SAS products themselves.

The main disadvantage to the autocall facility is that the macro program must be compiled the first time it is used in a SAS session. This takes resources. Also, resources are used to search the autocall libraries for the macro program reference.

After the macro processor finds your macro program in your autocall library, it submits the macro program for compilation. If there are any macro language statements in open code, these statements are immediately executed. The macro program is compiled and stored in the session compiled macro program catalog, SASMACR, just as if you submitted it yourself. SASMACR is in the WORK directory.

The macro program may be reused within your SAS session. When it is, only the macro program itself is executed. Any macro language statements in open code that may have been stored with the macro program are not executed again.

The compiled macro program is deleted at the end of the session when the catalog, WORK.SASMACR, is deleted. The code remains in the autocall library.

Creating an Autocall Library

The macro programs that you select for your autocall library can be stored as external files or as SOURCE entries in SAS catalogs.

To store macro programs as external files in a directory-based system such as Windows, OpenVMS, and UNIX, you define the directory and add the macro programs to the directory. Each macro program is stored in an individual file with a file type or extension of SAS. The name given to the file must be the same as the macro program name.

Under MVS, macro programs that are stored as external files are saved as members of a partitioned data set. The name of the member should be the same as the name of the macro program.

Under CMS, macro programs that are stored as external files are saved as members of a MACLIB. The name of the member should be the same as the name of the macro program.

When storing macro programs in a SAS catalog, make each macro program a separate SOURCE entry. The name of the SOURCE entry should be the same as the macro program name.

Figure 8.1 shows a Windows 95 directory containing four macro programs.

Figure 8.1   A Windows 95 directory containing autocall macro programs

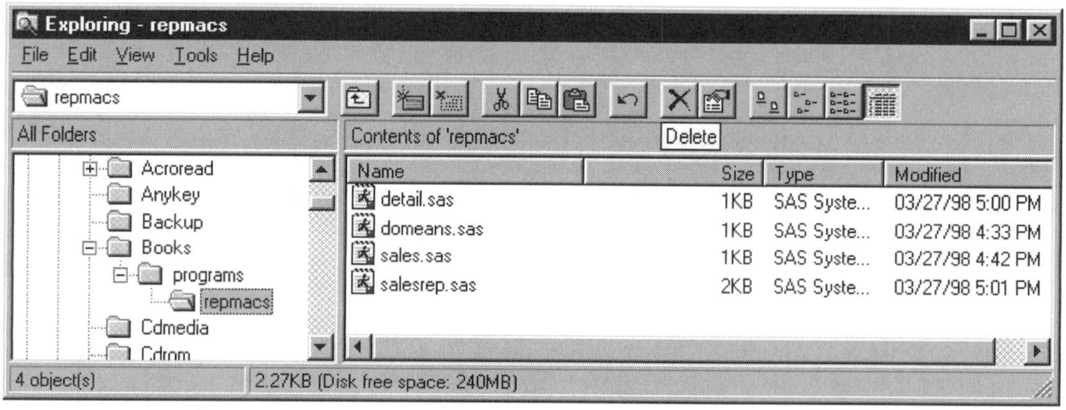

The next figure shows a SAS catalog that contains the four macro programs stored as SOURCE entries (Figure 8.2).

Figure 8.2   A SAS catalog containing autocall macro programs stored as SOURCE entries

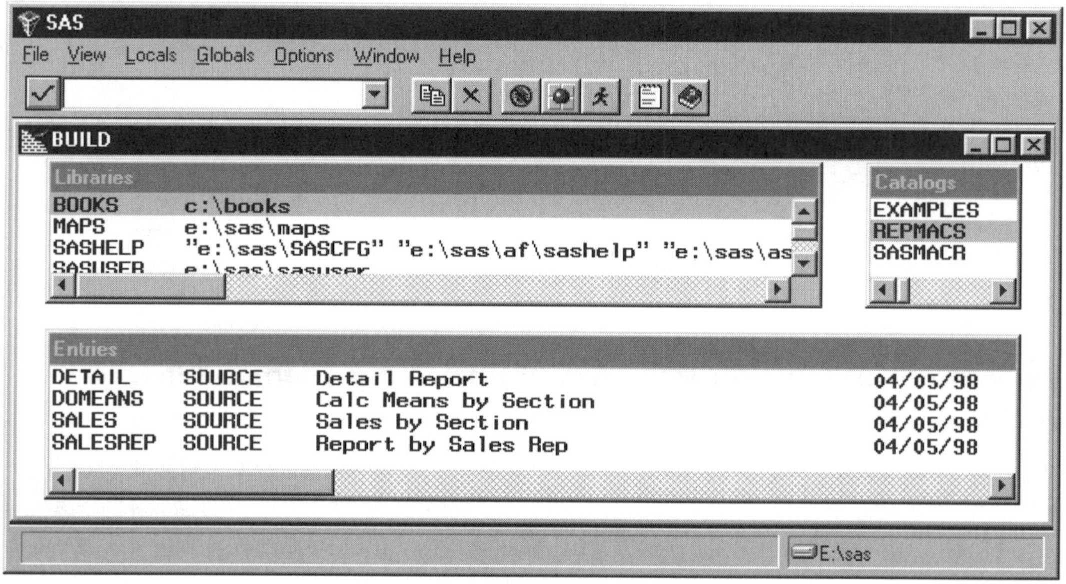

Making Autocall Libraries Available to Your Programs

When you want the SAS System to search for your macro programs in autocall libraries, you must specify the two SAS options, MAUTOSOURCE and SASAUTOS. These options can be specified three ways:

- add MAUTOSOURCE and SASAUTOS to the SAS command when starting the SAS session

- submit an OPTIONS statement with MAUTOSOURCE and SASAUTOS from within a SAS program

- submit an OPTIONS statement with MAUTOSOURCE and SASAUTOS from within an interactive SAS session.

The MAUTOSOURCE option must be enabled to tell the macro processor to search autocall libraries when resolving macro program references. To turn off MAUTOSOURCE, specify NOMAUTOSOURCE. Having MAUTOSOURCE disabled when you are not using autocall libraries saves computing time.

```
options mautosource;

options nomautosource;
```

The SASAUTOS option identifies the location of the autocall libraries to the macro processor. On the SASAUTOS option, specify either the actual directory reference or the filerefs that point to the directories. A FILENAME statement defines the fileref.

The syntax of SASAUTOS follows. The first line shows how to specify one library. The second line shows how to specify multiple libraries. The macro processor searches the libraries in the order in which they are listed on the SASAUTOS option.

```
options sasautos=library;

options sasautos=(library-1, library-2,..., library-n);
```

Defining Filerefs under Windows 95 and Using Them to Identify Autocall Libraries

The next statements define two filerefs under Windows 95 with SAS Release 6.12 and assigns them to SASAUTOS.

```
filename reports 'c:\books\programs\repmacs';
filename graphs 'c:\books\programs\grphmacs';
options sasautos=(reports graphs);
```

Explicitly Specifying the Directory Locations of Autocall Libraries on the OPTIONS Statement

To specify the same libraries without using filerefs, submit the following statement:

```
options sasautos=
    ('c:\books\programs\repmacs' 'c:\books\programs\grphmacs');
```

Identifying Autocall Libraries That are Stored in SAS Catalogs

An autocall library stored in a SAS catalog requires a parameter on the FILENAME statement that identifies the autocall library. The syntax of the FILENAME statement is

```
filename fileref catalog 'library.catalog';
```

The next statements reference an autocall library stored in a SAS catalog under Windows 95 SAS Version 6.12.

```
filename mymacs catalog 'books.repmacs';
options sasautos=mymacs;
```

Listing the Names of the Autocall Libraries that are Defined in the SAS Session

If you want to check what autocall libaries are defined, submit the following PROC step.

```
proc options option=sasautos;
run;
```

The Autocall Facility under Windows, OS/2, and Other Directory-Based Systems

Under a directory-based system, all macro programs are stored as individual files in a directory. Each of the macro programs should have a file extension of .SAS and a file name identical to the macro program name. Examples in the previous section use the autocall facility under Windows 95.

The Autocall Facility under OS/390 (MVS) Batch

Under the OS/390 operating system, autocall libraries are stored in partitioned data sets. Each macro program is a member in the partitioned data set. The name of the member is the same as the name of the macro program. A JCL DD statement assigns autocall libraries. The following example shows the beginning of the JCL for a batch job that specifies one autocall library. Note that the MAUTOSOURCE option is enabled.

```
//MYJOB    JOB  account....
//         EXEC SAS,OPTIONS='MAUTOSOURCE'
//SASAUTOS DD   DSN=BOOKS.REPMACS,DISP=SHR
```

The next example shows how multiple macro libraries can be specified.

```
//MYJOB    JOB  account....
//         EXEC SAS,OPTIONS='MAUTOSOURCE'
//SASAUTOS DD   DSN=BOOKS.REPMACS,DISP=SHR
//         DD   DSN=BOOKS.GRPHMACS,DISP=SHR
```

An OPTIONS statement can also be submitted from within the SAS program to specify the use of autocall libraries. The following statement specifies one autocall library.

```
options mautosource sasautos='books.repmacs';
```

The following statement specifies two autocall libraries.

```
options mautosource sasautos=
                ('books.repmacs' 'books.grphmacs');
```

The Autocall Facility under TSO

As with OS/390 batch jobs, autocall libraries under TSO are stored in partitioned data sets with each macro program a member of the set.

The following example starts an interactive TSO session that assigns an autocall library.

```
sas options('mautosource sasautos="books.repmacs"')
```

The next example starts an interactive TSO session that assigns two autocall libraries.

```
sas options('mautosource
    sasautos=("books.repmacs" "books.grphmacs")')
```

Autocall libraries can also be specified from within the SAS session by using the OPTIONS statement. The OPTIONS statement is written as shown in the OS/390 Batch section above.

The Autocall Facility under UNIX

As with other directory-based systems, autocall libraries under UNIX are made up of separate files each with the extension .SAS. Each macro program is in a separate file. The name of the file is the same as the name of the macro program.

The following example specifies one autocall library.

```
sas -mautosource -sasautos '/books/programs/repmacs'
```

The next example specifies two autocall libraries.

```
sas -mautosource -sasautos '/books/programs/grphmacs' -sasautos
'/books/programs/repmacs'
```

From within a UNIX SAS session, the following line specifies one autocall library.

```
options mautosource sasautos='/books/programs/repmacs'
```

The next OPTIONS statement specifies two autocall libraries from within a UNIX SAS session.

```
options mautosource sasautos=
('/books/programs/repmacs','/books/programs/grphmacs');
```

The Autocall Facility under OpenVMS

OpenVMS is a directory-based operating system. Macro programs in an autocall library are stored in a directory as separate files. The name of the file is the same as the name of the macro program. The extension of the macro program files should be .SAS.

The following SAS command specifies one autocall library.

```
sas /mautosource/sasautos='[books.programs.repmacs]'
```

The next SAS command specifies two autocall libraries.

```
sas /mautosource/sasautos=
('[books.programs.repmacs]', '[books.programs.grphmacs]')
```

From within a SAS program or SAS interactive session, the following OPTIONS statement can be submitted to specify one autocall library.

```
options mautosource sasautos='[books.programs.repmacs]';
```

The next OPTIONS statement can be submitted to specify two autocall libraries.

```
options mautosource sasautos=
('[books.programs.repmacs]', '[books.programs.grphmacs]');
```

Accessing the Autocall Macros That Come with the SAS System

Autocall libraries of macro programs come with many of the SAS products. You can use these macro programs in your SAS programs. A variety of macro programs come with base SAS. Some of the applications include changing the case of a macro variable value and formatting procedure output as HTML pages.

To find out what autocall libraries you have available, check the filerefs that are defined when your SAS session is initialized. For example, from a Windows session, enter the FILENAME command. You should see a SASAUTOS filename and several directories of macro programs. Also, check to see if MAUTOSOURCE is enabled. If not, turn the option on so that you may reference macro programs in the SAS System autocall libraries.

To find out the macro programs available in a SAS System autocall library, look at the file list of macro programs in the directory that contains the macro programs. Then use an editor to view the macro programs that interest you.

For example, under Windows 95, when the SAS System is installed in the c:\sas directory, the base SAS macro programs are in the c:\sas\core\sasmacro directory. Documentation at the beginning of each macro program describes how to use the macro program.

One macro program in the c:\sas\core\sasmacro directory is %LOWCASE. The %LOWCASE macro program converts the parameter to lower case. Following is an example of using %LOWCASE.

```
options mautosource;
%put %lowcase(ABCD);
%put %lowcase(MAKE THIS LOWERCASE);
```

The SAS log looks as follows after the above code is submitted.

```
5      options mautosource;
6      %put %lowcase(ABCD);
abcd
7      %put %lowcase(MAKE THIS LOWERCASE);
make this lowercase
```

Saving Macro Programs with the Stored Compiled Macro Facility

Macro programs that you want to save and do not expect to modify can be compiled and saved in SAS catalogs using the stored compiled macro facility. When a compiled macro program is referenced in a SAS program, the macro processor skips the compiling step, retrieves the compiled macro program, and executes the compiled code.

The main advantage of this facility is that it prevents repeated compiling of macro programs that are frequently used.

A disadvantage of this facility is that the compiled versions of macro programs cannot be moved to other operating systems. The macro source code must be saved and recompiled under the new operating system. Further, if you are moving the compiled macro programs to a different release of SAS under the same operating system, you may also have to recompile the macro programs.

Macro source code is not stored with the compiled macro program. A compiled macro program cannot be reverse engineered to obtain the macro source code. You are responsible for maintaining a copy of the macro source code. A convenient place to store the code is an autocall library.

Setting SAS Options to Create Stored Compiled Macro Programs

Two SAS options must be set before you can compile and store your macro programs: MSTORED and SASMSTORE.

The MSTORED option instructs the SAS System that you want to make stored compiled macro programs available to your SAS session. The OPTIONS statement with MSTORED looks as follows.

```
options mstored;
```

To turn off the MSTORED option, submit the following OPTIONS statement.

```
options nomstored;
```

The value that is assigned to the SASMSTORE option is the libref that points to the SAS catalog containing the compiled macro programs. A LIBNAME statement is used to define the libref. An example of SASMSTORE under Windows 95 in SAS Release 6.12 follows:

```
libname myapps 'c:\books\programs';
options mstored sasmstore=myapps;
```

The SAS System writes compiled macro programs to a catalog called SASMACR. The SASMACR catalog is stored in the directory specified by the SASMSTORE option. Do not rename this catalog. Use the CATALOG command or PROC CATALOG to view the list of macro programs stored in this catalog.

Creating Stored Compiled Macro Programs

Once the SAS options in the previous section are set, macro programs can be compiled and stored in a catalog by adding options to the %MACRO statement. The syntax of %MACRO when you want to compile and store a macro program follows:

```
%macro macro-name(parameters) / store des="description";
  macro-program-code
%mend macro-name;
```

The STORE keyword is required. The DES= option is not required. With DES=, you can provide up to 40 characters of text to describe your macro program. This text is then displayed when you view the contents of the catalog that holds the compiled stored macro programs. An example of defining a macro program and storing it in a catalog under Windows 95 in SAS Release 6.12 follows:

```
libname libname myapps 'c:\books\programs';
options mstored sasmstore=myapps;

%macro reptitle(repprog) / store des='Standard Report Titles';
   title "Bookstore Report &repprog";
   title2 "Processing Date: &sysdate  SAS Version: &sysver";
%mend reptitle;
```

Working with the Catalog that Contains Stored Compiled Macro Programs

PROC CATALOG and the CATALOG window can manage the catalog that contains the stored compiled macro programs.

A PROC CATALOG step to list the macro programs stored in the previous example follows:

```
libname myapps 'c:\books\programs';
proc catalog c=myapps.sasmacr;
   contents;
run;
quit;
```

If REPTITLE is the only macro in the MYAPPS.SASMACR catalog, the OUTPUT from the PROC CATALOG step looks like the example in Figure 8.3.

Figure 8.3   Output from PROC CATALOG after storing a compiled macro program

```
                    The SAS System                              1

                Contents of Catalog BOOKS.SASMACR

    #  Name        Type       Date        Description

    1  REPTITLE    MACRO      03/08/99    Standard Report Titles
```

Resolving Macro Program References When Using the Autocall Facility and the Stored Compiled Macro Facility

The autocall facility and the stored compiled macro facility have increased the scope of the tasks that the macro processor can do for you. Now instead of explicitly submitting a macro program, you tell the macro processor where and how the macro program is stored. The macro processor understands that it should check these sources after looking within the SAS session for macro programs that were compiled during the session.

If the macro processor finds the macro program in your autocall library, it submits the macro program for compilation. When the macro processor finds the macro program in your SASMACR catalog, it submits for execution the compiled code that is stored in the catalog.

When you make autocall libraries and stored compiled macro programs available to your SAS session by enabling the options described above, the macro processor takes the steps in Figure 8.4 to resolve a macro program reference.

Figure 8.4   **How the macro processor resolves calls to macro programs**

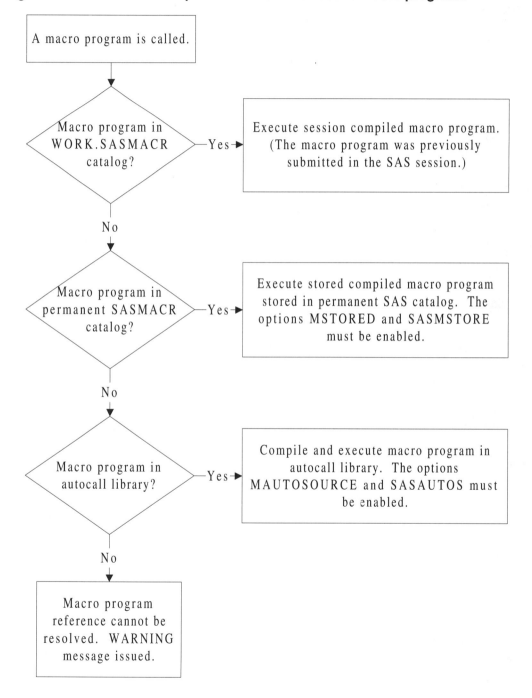

A Stepwise Method for Writing Macro Programs

By now, you've probably thought of at least one application that you could rewrite as a macro program. You've written the DATA steps and the PROC steps and you'd like to reuse this code. You've noticed ways that it can be generalized into a macro program.

After you decide an application is appropriate to write as a macro program, build the macro program in steps. Developing your macro program in steps of increasing complexity ensures that your macro program ends up doing exactly what you want it to do. It is also easier to debug a macro program as you develop it.

This chapter describes the steps in taking SAS programming requests and writing a macro program to handle the requests. An example illustrates the process.

Building a Macro Program in Four Steps

The four basic steps in building a macro program are

1. **Write, test, and debug the SAS program(s) that you want the macro program to build.**
   Do not use any macro variables or macro language statements in this step.

2. **Remove hard-coded programming constants from the program(s) in Step 1.**
   Replace these constants with macro variables. Hard-coded programming constants are items like the values on a WHERE statement. Use %LET statements in open code to define the macro variables. Test and debug the program(s). Use the SYMBOLGEN option to verify the results of using the macro variables.

3. **Create macro program(s) from the program(s) in Step 2.**
   Add parameters to the macro program(s) if appropriate. Test with different parameters. Use the SAS options MPRINT and SYMBOLGEN to review the results of processing this macro program.

4. **Refine and generalize the macro program(s) in Step 3 by adding macro language statements like %IF-%THEN and %DO groups.**
   After several macro programs are tested in Step 3, write programming statements to combine the macro programs into one macro program. Test the macro programming logic. Use the SAS options MPRINT, SYMBOLGEN, and MLOGIC to verify that your macro program works correctly.

Applying the Four Steps to an Example

Suppose that you have the on-going task of producing sales reports for the computer books department of the bookstore using the year-to-date sales data set. These reports vary, but several items in the reports are the same and the layout of the reports is the same. To save yourself coding time each time a report is requested, you decide to develop a macro program that contains the framework of the reports. Parameters that are passed to the macro program and macro language statements within the macro program customize the basic report.

Your macro program should be able to display the following:

- Sales overall.

- Sales by section.

- Sales by month of sale.

- Sales by sales representative.

- Sales by combinations of the three "BY" variables above.

- All of the above within a specific date range; by default the date range is from the beginning of the year to the current date.

- Pie charts of sales by section when they are processed for a full year or for quarters.

- Analyses for any or all of the sales variables: cost, listpric, salepric, profit.

The rest of this chapter uses the four steps to build a macro program that will generate the reports above.

Step 1: Write, test, and debug the SAS program(s) that you want the macro program to build

Many separate reports are requested above. Three of them follow. The three programs will be referred to as Report A, Report B, and Report C. These three programs are used to design the macro program.

Program for Report A with No Macro Facility Features

The Report A program calculates totals for sales information from the beginning of the year through a specified date. In the example, the report is through November 13, 1998. The variables that are analyzed are cost, list price, sale price, and profit.

```
*----REPORT A;
options pageno=1;
title "Sales Report";
title2 "01JAN1998 through 13NOV1998";
data temp;
   set books.ytdsales(where=
                     ('01jan1998'd le datesold le '13nov1998'd));
   mosale=month(datesold);
   profit=salepric-cost;
   label profit='Profit'
         mosale='Month of Sale';
run;

proc tabulate data=temp;
   var cost listpric salepric profit;
   tables n*f=6.
          (cost listpric salepric profit)*sum*f=dollar10.2;
   keylabel n='Titles Sold';
run;
```

Output for Report A is in Figure 9.1.

Figure 9.1   Output for Report A

```
                        Sales Report                          1
                  01JAN1998 through 13NOV1998

    -----------------------------------------------------
    |       |Wholesale |          |          |           |
    |       |     Cost |List Price|Sale Price|  Profit   |
    |Titles |----------+----------+----------+-----------|
    | Sold  |   SUM    |   SUM    |   SUM    |   SUM     |
    |-------+----------+----------+----------+-----------|
    |  5847 |$128041.24|$180870.65|$176830.71|$48,789.46 |
    -----------------------------------------------------
```

Program for Report B with No Macro Facility Features

Report B analyzes sales for the first quarter. The tables and charts analyze sale price and profit.

```
*----REPORT B;
options pageno=1;
title "Sales Report";
title2 "01JAN1998 through 31MAR1998";
data temp;
   set books.ytdsales(where=
                  ('01jan1998'd le datesold le '31mar1998'd));
   mosale=month(datesold);
   profit=salepric-cost;
   label profit='Profit'
         mosale='Month of Sale';
run;

proc tabulate data=temp;
   title3 "Sales for Quarter";
   class section;
   var salepric profit;
   tables section all,
     n*f=6. (salepric profit)*sum*f=dollar10.2;
   keylabel all='Total Sales'
            n='Titles Sold';
run;

proc gchart data=temp;
   title3 "Sales for Quarter";
   pie section / type=sum sumvar=salepric
                 coutline=black percent=arrow;
   run;
   pie section / type=sum sumvar=profit
                 coutline=black percent=arrow;
   run;
quit;
```

Output for Report B is in figure 9.2.

Figure 9.2   Output for Report B

```
                        Sales Report                         1
               01JAN1998 through 31MAR1998
                    Sales for Quarter


       ---------------------------------------------
       |               |      |Sale Price|  Profit  |
       |               |Titles|----------+----------|
       |               | Sold |   SUM    |   SUM    |
       |-------------+------+----------+----------|
       |Section        |      |          |          |
       |-------------|      |          |          |
       |Internet       |  340|$10,331.30| $2,856.04|
       |-------------+------+----------+----------|
       |Networks and   |      |          |          |
       |Communication |  140| $4,092.75| $1,133.21|
       |-------------+------+----------+----------|
       |Operating      |      |          |          |
       |Systems       |  415|$12,643.62| $3,482.41|
       |-------------+------+----------+----------|
       |Programming    |      |          |          |
       |Languages     |  180| $5,343.39| $1,478.96|
       |-------------+------+----------+----------|
       |Web Design     |  380|$11,540.42| $3,180.68|
       |-------------+------+----------+----------|
       |Total Sales    | 1455|$43,951.49|$12,131.30|
       ---------------------------------------------
```

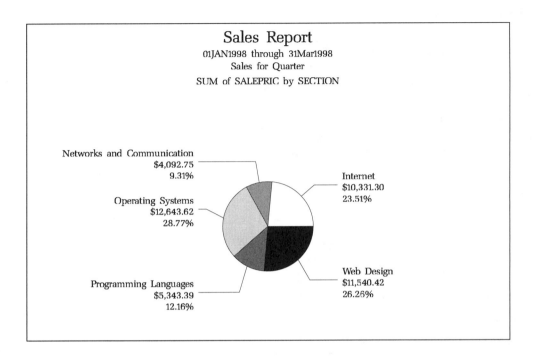

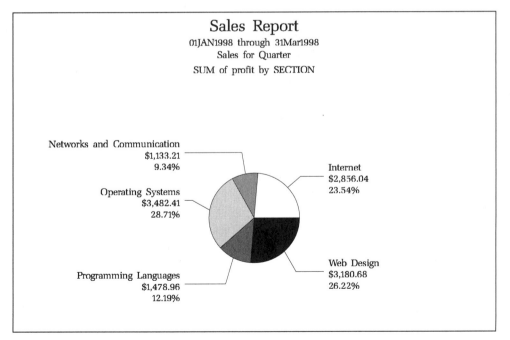

Program for Report C with No Macro Facility Features

Report C analyzes information from the beginning of the year to the current date for cost, list price, sale price, and profit. The information is summarized by section and sales representative. The current date for the example is November 24, 1998.

```
*----REPORT C;
options pageno=1;
title "Sales Report";
title2 "01JAN1998 through 24NOV1998";
data temp;
   set books.ytdsales(where=
                      ('01jan1998'd le datesold le '24nov1998'd));
   mosale=month(datesold);
   profit=salepric-cost;
   label profit='Profit'
         mosale='Month of Sale'
         saleinit='Inits';
run;

proc tabulate data=temp;
   class section saleinit;
   var cost listpric salepric profit;
   tables section*(saleinit all) all,
     n*f=6. (cost listpric salepric profit)*sum*f=dollar10.2;
   keylabel all='Total Sales'
            n='Titles Sold';
run;
```

Output for Report C is in Figure 9.3.

Figure 9.3   Output for Report C

```
                          Sales Report                           1
                  01JAN1998 through 24NOV1998
```

		Titles Sold	Wholesale Cost SUM	List Price SUM	Sale Price SUM	Profit SUM
Section	Inits					
Intern-et	BLT	637	$13,975.04	$19,732.15	$19,296.65	$5,321.61
	JMB	513	$11,251.67	$15,917.35	$15,556.13	$4,304.47
	MJM	414	$9,158.23	$12,923.30	$12,622.98	$3,464.75
	Total Sales	1564	$34,384.93	$48,572.80	$47,475.75	$13,090.82
Networ-ks and Commun-ication	Inits					
	BLT	238	$5,060.67	$7,136.10	$6,980.26	$1,919.59
	JMB	174	$3,787.17	$5,375.30	$5,268.57	$1,481.40
	MJM	154	$3,369.24	$4,750.30	$4,636.09	$1,266.85
	Total Sales	566	$12,217.07	$17,261.70	S16,884.93	$4,667.86
Operat-ing Systems	Inits					
	BLT	654	$14,276.15	$20,160.30	S19,656.93	$5,380.78
	JMB	553	$12,188.00	$17,185.35	S16,833.63	$4,645.64
	MJM	445	$9,854.67	$13,929.75	S13,659.69	$3,805.02
	Total Sales	1652	$36,318.81	$51,275.40	S50,150.24	$13,831.44
Progra-mming Langua-ges	Inits					
	BLT	307	$6,657.85	$9,419.65	$9,210.09	$2,552.24
	JMB	282	$6,086.71	$8,588.90	$8,406.60	$2,319.89
	MJM	197	$4,215.83	$5,953.15	$5,820.88	$1,605.05

```
(CONTINUED)

                          Sales Report                          2
                01JAN1998 through 24NOV1998

---------------------------------------------------------------------
|          |        |Wholesale |          |          |          |
|          |        |    Cost  |List Price|Sale Price|  Profit  |
|          |Titles|-----------+----------+----------+----------|
|          | Sold |    SUM   |   SUM    |   SUM    |   SUM    |
|----------+------+----------+----------+----------+----------|
|Section|Total    |          |          |          |          |
|-------|Sales    |          |          |          |          |
|Progra-|         |          |          |          |          |
|mming  |         |          |          |          |          |
|Langua-|         |          |          |          |          |
|ges    |      786|$16,960.39|$23,961.70|$23,437.58| $6,477.19|
|-------+------+----------+----------+----------+----------|
|Web    |Inits |          |          |          |          |
|Design |------|          |          |          |          |
|       |BLT   |      604|$13,305.18|$18,764.80|$18,352.67| $5,047.49|
|       |------+------+----------+----------+----------+----------|
|       |JMB   |      518|$11,435.77|$16,154.10|$15,777.10| $4,341.33|
|       |------+------+----------+----------+----------+----------|
|       |MJM   |      390| $8,523.73|$12,063.50|$11,816.89| $3,293.16|
|       |------+------+----------+----------+----------+----------|
|       |Total |          |          |          |          |
|       |Sales |     1512|$33,264.67|$46,982.40|$45,946.65|$12,681.98|
|----------+------+----------+----------+----------+----------|
|Total Sales     |     6080|$133145.87|$188054.00|$183895.15|$50,749.28|
---------------------------------------------------------------------
```

After running these three programs and verifying that they display the information required, move on to Step 2.

Step 2: Remove hard-coded programming constants from the program(s) in Step 1

When you review the three programs created in Step 1, some patterns emerge:

- Observations are selected within a certain range of sales dates. This range is specified in the WHERE clause in the DATA step and in the titles.

- Analysis variables are selected from a defined set of variables.

- Grouping variables are selected from a defined set of variables.

The values in the above list are hard-coded programming constants in the three programs from Step 1. Macro variables can be created in open code to hold these values.

Program for Report A with Step 2 Modifications

A revised Report A program follows. The inserted %LET statements and macro variable references are highlighted.

```
*----REPORT A;
%let repyear=1998;
%let start=01Jan&repyear;
%let stop=13Nov&repyear;
%let vars=cost listpric salepric profit;

options pageno=1 symbolgen;

title "Sales Report";
title2 "&start through &stop";
data temp;
   set books.ytdsales(where=
        ("&start"d le datesold le "&stop"d));
   mosale=month(datesold);
   profit=salepric-cost;
   label profit='Profit'
         mosale='Month of Sale';
run;

proc tabulate data=temp;
   var &vars;
   tables n*f=6.
          (&vars)*sum*f=dollar10.2;
   keylabel n='Titles Sold';
run;
```

Program for Report B with Step 2 Modifications

Report B is modified to contain macro variables. Some of the changes that were made to this program are made to the Report A program as well.

```
*----Report B;
%let repyear=1998;
%let start=01Jan&repyear;
%let stop=31Mar&repyear;

%let classvar=section;
%let vars=salepric profit;

options pageno=1 symbolgen;

title "Sales Report";
title2 "&start through &stop";
```

```
data temp;
   set books.ytdsales(where=
        ("&start"d le datesold le "&stop"d));
   mosale=month(datesold);
   profit=salepric-cost;
   label profit='Profit'
         mosale='Month of Sale';
run;

proc tabulate data=temp;
   title3 "Sales for Quarter";
   class &classvar;
   var &vars;
   tables &classvar all,
      n*f=6. (&vars)*sum*f=dollar10.2;
   keylabel all='Total Sales'
            n='Titles Sold';
run;

proc gchart data=temp;
   title3 "Sales for Quarter";
   pie &classvar / type=sum sumvar=%scan(&vars,1)
                   coutline=black percent=arrow;
   run;
   pie &classvar / type=sum sumvar=%scan(&vars,2)
                   coutline=black percent=arrow;

   run;
quit;
```

Program for Report C with Step 2 Modifications

Report C is modified with the creation of macro variables in open code. The features added to this program are similar to those added to the Report A program and the Report B program.

```
*----REPORT C;
%let repyear=1998;
%let start=01Jan&repyear;
%let stop=24Nov&repyear;

%let classvar=section saleinit;
%let vars=cost listpric salepric profit;

options pageno=1 symbolgen;

title "Sales Report";
title2 "&start through &stop";
data temp;
   set books.ytdsales(where=
      ("&start"d le datesold le "&stop"d));
```

```
    mosale=month(datesold);
    profit=salepric-cost;
    label profit='Profit'
          mosale='Month of Sale';
 run;

 proc tabulate data=temp;
    class &classvar;
    var &vars;
    tables %scan(&classvar,1)*
      (%scan(&classvar,2) all) all,
       n*f=6. (&vars)*sum*f=dollar10.2;
    keylabel all='Total Sales'
             n='Titles Sold';
 run;
```

Step 3: Create macro program(s) from the program(s) in Step 2

In Step 2, similar changes were made to each of the three programs. Macro variables were defined for the range in dates that were selected from the data set. Macro variables were defined to hold the classification variables and analysis variables.

The temptation may be to jump to writing %DO blocks and conditional processing statements, but first complete Step 3. In Step 3, define macro programs that use parameters. The parameters to the macro programs will usually be the macro variables that were defined in Step 2. By not including macro language statements in these macro program definitions, you'll be sure that the parameters you define execute correctly.

Use the SYMBOLGEN and MPRINT options to verify that your programming changes do what you intend.

Program for Report A with Step 3 Modifications

Report A is converted to a macro program as follows. Four keyword parameters are defined. Three parameters—the start date, the stop date, and the analysis variables—are defined with default values.

```
 options symbolgen mprint;

%macro reporta(repyear=,start=01JAN,stop=31DEC,
               vars=cost listpric salepric profit);
    options pageno=1;

    %let start=&start&repyear;
    %let stop=&stop&repyear;
```

```
title "Sales Report";
title2 "&start through &stop";
data temp;
   set books.ytdsales(where=
      ("&start"d le datesold le "&stop"d));
   mosale=month(datesold);
   profit=salepric-cost;
   label profit='Profit'
         mosale='Month of Sale';
run;

proc tabulate data=temp;
   var &vars;
   tables n*f=6.
          (&vars)*sum*f=dollar10.2;
   keylabel n='Titles Sold';
run;
%mend reporta;
```

The code to call REPORTA now becomes

   %reporta(repyear=1998,stop=13NOV)

The start date for the call to REPORTA is the default value of January 1. The stop date that is required to produce REPORTA is November 13. Since the default stop date is December 31, the stop date parameter must be specified. The analysis variables are the same as the default set of variables that were listed in the macro program definition for REPORTA. The VARS parameter is not specified.

Program for Report B with Step 2 Modifications

Report B is converted into a macro program as follows. Five keyword parameters are defined. Two parameters, the start date and the stop date, are defined with default values.

```
options symbolgen mprint;

%macro reportb(repyear=,start=01JAN,stop=31DEC,
               classvar=,vars=);
   options pageno=1;

   %let start=&start&repyear;
   %let stop=&stop&repyear;

   title "Sales Report";
   title2 "&start through &stop";
   data temp;
      set books.ytdsales(where=
         ("&start"d le datesold le &stop"d));
```

```
      mosale=month(datesold);
      profit=salepric-cost;
      label profit='Profit'
            mosale='Month of Sale';
   run;

   proc tabulate data=temp;
      title3 "Sales for Quarter";
      class &classvar;
      var &vars;
      tables &classvar all,
        n*f=6. (&vars)*sum*f=dollar10.2;
      keylabel all='Total Sales'
               n='Titles Sold';
   run;

   proc gchart data=temp;
      title3 "Sales for Quarter";
      pie &classvar / type=sum sumvar=%scan(&vars,1)
                      coutline=black percent=arrow;
      run;
      pie &classvar / type=sum sumvar=%scan(&vars,2)
                      coutline=black percent=arrow;
      run;
   quit;
%mend reportb;
```

The call to REPORTB is written as follows:

```
%reportb(repyear=1998,stop=31Mar,classvar=section,
         vars=salepric profit)
```

The start date for the call to REPORTB is the default value of January 1. The stop date that is required to produce Report B is March 31. Since the default stop date is December 31, the stop date parameter must be specified. The information in the report is summarized by the classification variable, SECTION. Two analysis variables are specified: SALEPRIC and PROFIT.

Program for Report C with Step 2 Modifications

Next, Report C is converted into a macro program. Five keyword parameters are defined. Three parameters—the start date, the stop date, and the analysis variables—are defined with default values.

```
options symbolgen mprint;

%macro reportc(repyear=,start=01JAN,stop=31DEC,
               classvar=,vars=cost listpric salepric profit);
   options pageno=1;

   %let start=&start&repyear;
```

```
%let stop=&stop&repyear;

title "Sales Report";
title2 "&start through &stop";
data temp;
   set books.ytdsales(where=
      ("&start"d le datesold le "&stop"d));
   mosale=month(datesold);
   profit=salepric-cost;
   label profit='Profit'
         mosale='Month of Sale'
         saleinit='Inits';
run;

proc tabulate data=temp;
   class &classvar;
   var &vars;
   tables %scan(&classvar,1)*
          (%scan(&classvar,2) all) all,
          n*f=6. (&vars)*sum*f=dollar10.2;
   keylabel all='Total Sales'
            n='Titles Sold';
run;
%mend reportc;
```

The call to REPORTC looks as follows:

```
%reportc(repyear=1998,stop=24NOV,classvar=section saleinit)
```

The start date for the call to REPORTC is the default value of January 1. The stop date required to produce REPORTC is the current date of November 24 and must be specified since the default stop date is December 31. The information in the report is summarized by two classification variables, SECTION and SALEINIT. The analysis variables are the default set of variables that were defined in the macro program definition for REPORTC.

Step 4: Refine and generalize the macro program(s) in Step 3 by adding macro language statements like %IF-%THEN and %DO groups

The goal in Step 4 for the example application is to converge the three macro programs into one. The main similarity among the three programs is that they have most of the same parameters. Macro language statements are required to handle the following differences and to further generalize the programs:

- No classification variable is specified in Report A. One classification variable is specified in Report B. Two classification variables are specified in Report C.

- Reports A and C use all the analysis variables. Report B uses only two analysis variables.

- Report B is executed at the end of a quarter. Therefore, the third title is required for this report.

- The number of PIE statements in Report B is equal to the number of analysis variables.

An enhancement to add to the macro program is to add macro language statements to define a default for the report year and stop date of the reports. When no report year is entered, use the current year. If stop date is specified as a null value, use the current date as the stop date for the report.

Conditional processing steps and iterative processing steps are incorporated into the consolidated macro program. One way to write this macro program follows. The changes are highlighted. Comments are added to the macro program to describe the processing of the macro program.

```
options symbolgen mprint logic;

%macro report(repyear=,start=01JAN,stop=31DEC,
              classvar=,vars=cost listpric salepric profit);

   options pageno=1;

   %*----Check if a value was specified for report year.
         If no value specified,use current year;
   %if &repyear= %then %let repyear=
                %sysfunc(year(%sysfunc(today())));
   %*----Check if stop date specified.  If null, use
         current date as stop date;
   %if &stop= %then %let stop=%substr(&sysdate,1,5);

   %let start=&start&repyear;
   %let stop=&stop&repyear;

   title "Sales Report";
   title2 "&start through &stop";
   data temp;
      set books.ytdsales(where=
         ("&start"d le datesold le "&stop"d));
      mosale=month(datesold);
      profit=salepric-cost;
      label profit='Profit'
            mosale='Month of Sale'
            saleinit='Inits';
   run;

   proc tabulate data=temp;
      %*----Only submit a CLASS statement if there is a
            classification variable;
      %if &classvar ne %then %do;
         class &classvar;
      %end;
```

```
      var &vars;
      tables
        %if &classvar ne %then %do;
          %*---Determine leftmost row dimension variable;
          %let mainclas=%scan(&classvar,1);
          &mainclas
          %if %length(&mainclas) < %length(&classvar) %then %do;
            %*----If more than one classification variable, nest
                  remaining classification variables under the
                  first;
            %*----Use the substring function to extract
                  classification variables after the first;
            %let pos2=%index(&classvar,%scan(&classvar,2));

            %*----Add the rest of the classification vars;
            * ( %substr(&classvar,&pos2) all)

          %end;
          all,
        %end;
        n*f=6. (&vars)*sum*f=dollar10.2;
        keylabel all='Total Sales'
                 n='Titles Sold';
run;

%*----Check if date range is for a quarter or year;
%let strtmody=%upcase(%substr(&start,1,5));
%let stopmody=%upcase(%substr(&stop,1,5));
%if (&strtmody=01JAN and &stopmody=31MAR) or
    (&strtmody=01APR and &stopmody=30JUN) or
    (&strtmody=01JUL and &stopmody=30SEP) or
    (&strtmody=01OCT and &stopmody=31DEC) or
    (&strtmody=01JAN and &stopmody=31DEC) %then %do;

  %*----Special titles for Quarter and for Year;
  %if not (&strtmody eq 01JAN and &stopmody eq 31DEC)
         %then %do;
    title3 "Sales for Quarter";
  %end;
  %else %do;
    title3 "&repyear Annual Sales";
  %end;

  proc gchart data=temp;
    %*----For each analysis variable, do a pie chart;
    %let setchrt=1;
    %let chrtvar=%scan(&vars,1);
```

```
      %do %while (&chrtvar ne );
         pie &classvar / type=sum sumvar=&chrtvar
                         coutline=black percent=arrow;
         run;

         %let setchrt=%eval(&setchrt+1);
         %let chrtvar=%scan(&vars,&setchrt);
      %end;
   quit;
 %end;
%mend report;
```

In Step 4, the SYMBOLGEN, MPRINT, and MLOGIC options can verify that your macro program works correctly. After you have thoroughly checked your macro program, disable these options to save computing time.

Executing the REPORT macro program

Many types of reports can now be generated by the REPORT macro program, including Reports A, B, and C.

Obtaining the Contents of Report A Using the REPORT Macro Program

The first request to sum sales information from the beginning of the year through November 13, 1998 is as follows:

```
%report(repyear=1998,stop=13NOV)
```

After the macro processor resolves this call, the SAS log with MPRINT enabled is as follows:

```
516   %report(repyear=1998,stop=13NOV)
MPRINT(REPORT):    OPTIONS PAGENO=1;
MPRINT(REPORT):    TITLE "Sales Report";
MPRINT(REPORT):    TITLE2 "01JAN1998 through 13NOV1998";
MPRINT(REPORT):    DATA TEMP;
MPRINT(REPORT):    SET BOOKS.YTDSALES(WHERE= ("01JAN1998"d LE
DATESOLD LE "13NOV1998"d));
MPRINT(REPORT):    MOSALE=MONTH(DATESOLD);
MPRINT(REPORT):    PROFIT=SALEPRIC-COST;
MPRINT(REPORT):    LABEL PROFIT= 'Profit' MOSALE= 'Month of
Sale' SALEINIT= 'Inits';
MPRINT(REPORT):    ;
MPRINT(REPORT):    RUN;

NOTE: The data set WORK.TEMP has 5847 observations and 12
variables.
```

```
NOTE: The DATA statement used 1.53 seconds.


MPRINT(REPORT):    PROC TABULATE DATA=TEMP;
MPRINT(REPORT):    VAR COST LISTPRIC SALEPRIC PROFIT;
MPRINT(REPORT):    TABLES N*F=6. (COST LISTPRIC SALEPRIC
PROFIT)*SUM*F=DOLLAR10.2;
MPRINT(REPORT):    KEYLABEL ALL='Total Sales' N='Titles Sold';
MPRINT(REPORT):    RUN;

NOTE: The PROCEDURE TABULATE used 0.39 seconds.
```

The output for the first call to REPORT is in Figure 9.4. This output is identical to that in Figure 9.1.

Figure 9.4   **Output for the first call to REPORT which generates the information that was specified for Report A**

```
                            Sales Report                          1
                   01JAN1998 through 13NOV1998

      ---------------------------------------------------------
      |        |Wholesale |          |          |            |
      |        |    Cost  |List Price|Sale Price|   Profit   |
      |Titles  |----------+----------+----------+------------|
      | Sold   |   SUM    |   SUM    |   SUM    |    SUM     |
      |------+-----------+----------+----------+------------|
      |  5847|$128041.24|$180870.65|$176830.71|$48,789.46|
      ---------------------------------------------------------
```

Obtaining the Contents of Report B Using the REPORT Macro Program

The second request to REPORT should generate statistics for sale price and profit by section from January 1, 1998 through March 31, 1998. This time period encompasses the first quarter. Therefore, pie charts should also be produced. The call to REPORT looks as follows:

```
%report(repyear=1998,stop=31Mar,classvar=section,
        vars=salepric profit)
```

The SAS LOG of resolving this second call to REPORT is as follows.

```
517   %report(repyear=1998,stop=31Mar,classvar=section,
518           vars=salepric profit)
MPRINT(REPORT):    OPTIONS PAGENO=1;
MPRINT(REPORT):    TITLE "Sales Report";
MPRINT(REPORT):    TITLE2 "01JAN1998 through 31Mar1998";
```

```
MPRINT(REPORT):    DATA TEMP;
MPRINT(REPORT):     SET BOOKS.YTDSALES(WHERE= ("01JAN1998"d LE
DATESOLD LE "31Mar1998"d));
MPRINT(REPORT):     MOSALE=MONTH(DATESOLD);
MPRINT(REPORT):     PROFIT=SALEPRIC-COST;
MPRINT(REPORT):     LABEL PROFIT= 'Profit' MOSALE= 'Month of
Sale' SALEINIT= 'Inits';
MPRINT(REPORT):     ;
MPRINT(REPORT):     RUN;
```

NOTE: The data set WORK.TEMP has 1455 observations and 12
variables.
NOTE: The DATA statement used 0.66 seconds.

```
MPRINT(REPORT):     PROC TABULATE DATA=TEMP;
MPRINT(REPORT):     CLASS SECTION;
MPRINT(REPORT):     VAR SALEPRIC PROFIT;
MPRINT(REPORT):     TABLES SECTION ALL, N*F=6. (SALEPRIC
PROFIT)*SUM*F=DOLLAR10.2;
MPRINT(REPORT):     KEYLABEL ALL='Total Sales' N='Titles Sold';
MPRINT(REPORT):     RUN;
```

NOTE: The PROCEDURE TABULATE used 0.27 seconds.

```
MPRINT(REPORT):     TITLE3 "Sales for Quarter";
MPRINT(REPORT):     PROC GCHART DATA=TEMP;
MPRINT(REPORT):     PIE SECTION / TYPE=SUM SUMVAR=SALEPRIC
COUTLINE=BLACK PERCENT=ARROW;
MPRINT(REPORT):     RUN;
```

WARNING: The values of SECTION have been truncated to 16
characters.
```
MPRINT(REPORT):     PIE SECTION / TYPE=SUM SUMVAR=PROFIT
COUTLINE=BLACK PERCENT=ARROW;
MPRINT(REPORT):     RUN;
```

WARNING: The values of SECTION have been truncated to 16
characters.
```
MPRINT(REPORT):     QUIT;
```

NOTE: The PROCEDURE GCHART used 2.62 seconds.

The output for the second call to REPORT is in Figure 9.5. This output is identical to that in
Figure 9.2.

Figure 9.5   Output for the second call to REPORT which generates the information that was specified for Report B

```
                              Sales Report                          1
                       01JAN1998 through 31Mar1998

        -----------------------------------------------------
       |              |      |Sale Price|   Profit   |
       |              |Titles|----------+----------|
       |              | Sold |   SUM    |    SUM     |
       |--------------+------+----------+----------|
       |Section       |      |          |          |
       |--------------|      |          |          |
       |Internet      |  340 |$10,331.30| $2,856.04|
       |--------------+------+----------+----------|
       |Networks and  |      |          |          |
       |Communication |  140 | $4,092.75| $1,133.21|
       |--------------+------+----------+----------|
       |Operating     |      |          |          |
       |Systems       |  415 |$12,643.62| $3,482.41|
       |--------------+------+----------+----------|
       |Programming   |      |          |          |
       |Languages     |  180 | $5,343.39| $1,478.96|
       |--------------+------+----------+----------|
       |Web Design    |  380 |$11,540.42| $3,180.68|
       |--------------+------+----------+----------|
       |Total Sales   | 1455 |$43,951.49|$12,131.30|
        -----------------------------------------------------
```

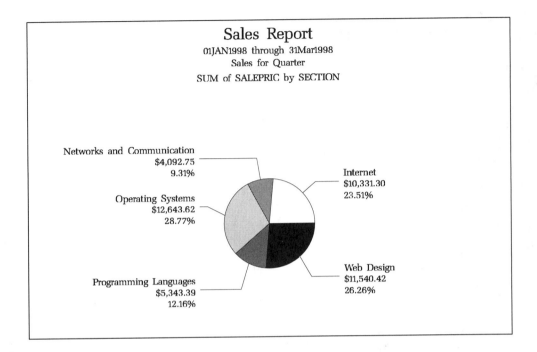

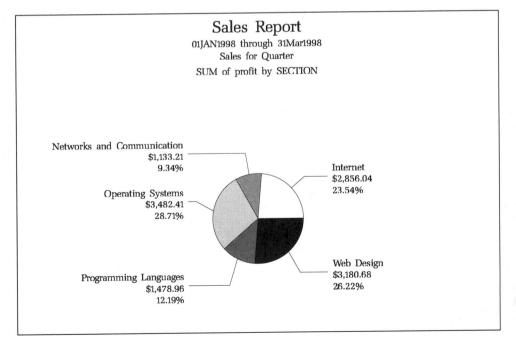

Obtaining the Contents of Report C Using the REPORT Macro Program

The third report summarizes sales information through the current date. The analysis is done by section and by sales representative. Assume the current date is November 24, 1998. The third call to REPORT is as follows:

```
%report(stop=,classvar=section saleinit)
```

The SAS log of resolving the third call to REPORT is as follows:

```
519   %report(stop=,classvar=section saleinit)
MPRINT(REPORT):    OPTIONS PAGENO=1;
MPRINT(REPORT):    TITLE "Sales Report";
MPRINT(REPORT):    TITLE2 "01JAN1998 through 24NOV1998";
MPRINT(REPORT):    DATA TEMP;
MPRINT(REPORT):    SET BOOKS.YTDSALES(WHERE= ("24NOV1998"d LE
DATESOLD LE "08APR1998"d));
MPRINT(REPORT):    MOSALE=MONTH(DATESOLD);
MPRINT(REPORT):    PROFIT=SALEPRIC-COST;
MPRINT(REPORT):    LABEL PROFIT= 'Profit' MOSALE= 'Month of
Sale' SALEINIT= 'Inits';
MPRINT(REPORT):    ;
MPRINT(REPORT):    RUN;

NOTE: The data set WORK.TEMP has 6080 observations and 12
variables.
NOTE: The DATA statement used 0.66 seconds.


MPRINT(REPORT):    PROC TABULATE DATA=TEMP;
MPRINT(REPORT):    CLASS SECTION SALEINIT;
MPRINT(REPORT):    VAR COST LISTPRIC SALEPRIC PROFIT;
MPRINT(REPORT):    TABLES SECTION * ( SALEINIT ALL) ALL, N*F=6.
(COST LISTPRIC SALEPRIC
PROFIT)*SUM*F=DOLLAR10.2;
MPRINT(REPORT):    KEYLABEL ALL='Total Sales' N='Titles Sold';
MPRINT(REPORT):    RUN;

NOTE: The PROCEDURE TABULATE used 0.77 seconds.
```

The output for the third call to REPORT is in Figure 9.6. This output is identical to that in Figure 9.3.

Figure 9.6   Output for the third call to REPORT, which generates the information that was specified for Report C

```
                              Sales Report                              1
                        01JAN1998 through 24Nov1998

----------------------------------------------------------------------------
|              |       |Wholesale |          |          |          |
|              |       |   Cost   |List Price|Sale Price|  Profit  |
|              |Titles |----------+----------+----------+----------|
|              | Sold  |  SUM     |   SUM    |   SUM    |   SUM    |
|--------------+-------+----------+----------+----------+----------|
|Section|Inits |       |          |          |          |          |
|-------+------|       |          |          |          |          |
|Intern-|BLT   |   637 |$13,975.04|$19,732.15|$19,296.65| $5,321.61|
|et     |------+-------+----------+----------+----------+----------|
|       |JMB   |   513 |$11,251.67|$15,917.35|$15,556.13| $4,304.47|
|       |------+-------+----------+----------+----------+----------|
|       |MJM   |   414 | $9,158.23|$12,923.30|$12,622.98| $3,464.75|
|       |------+-------+----------+----------+----------+----------|
|       |Total |       |          |          |          |          |
|       |Sales |  1564 |$34,384.93|$48,572.80|$47,475.75|$13,090.82|
|-------+------+-------+----------+----------+----------+----------|
|Networ-|Inits |       |          |          |          |          |
|ks and |------|       |          |          |          |          |
|Commun-|BLT   |   238 | $5,060.67| $7,136.10| $6,980.26| $1,919.59|
|ication|------+-------+----------+----------+----------+----------|
|       |JMB   |   174 | $3,787.17| $5,375.30| $5,268.57| $1,481.40|
|       |------+-------+----------+----------+----------+----------|
|       |MJM   |   154 | $3,369.24| $4,750.30| $4,636.09| $1,266.85|
|       |------+-------+----------+----------+----------+----------|
|       |Total |       |          |          |          |          |
|       |Sales |   566 |$12,217.07|$17,261.70|$16,884.93| $4,667.86|
|-------+------+-------+----------+----------+----------+----------|
|Operat-|Inits |       |          |          |          |          |
|ing    |------|       |          |          |          |          |
|Systems|BLT   |   654 |$14,276.15|$20,160.30|$19,656.93| $5,380.78|
|       |------+-------+----------+----------+----------+----------|
|       |JMB   |   553 |$12,188.00|$17,185.35|$16,833.63| $4,645.64|
|       |------+-------+----------+----------+----------+----------|
|       |MJM   |   445 | $9,854.67|$13,929.75|$13,659.69| $3,805.02|
|       |------+-------+----------+----------+----------+----------|
|       |Total |       |          |          |          |          |
|       |Sales |  1652 |$36,318.81|$51,275.40|$50,150.24|$13,831.44|
|-------+------+-------+----------+----------+----------+----------|
|Progra-|Inits |       |          |          |          |          |
|mming  |------|       |          |          |          |          |
|Langua-|BLT   |   307 | $6,657.85| $9,419.65| $9,210.09| $2,552.24|
|ges    |------+-------+----------+----------+----------+----------|
|       |JMB   |   282 | $6,086.71| $8,588.90| $8,406.60| $2,319.89|
|       |------+-------+----------+----------+----------+----------|
|       |MJM   |   197 | $4,215.83| $5,953.15| $5,820.88| $1,605.05|
----------------------------------------------------------------------------
```

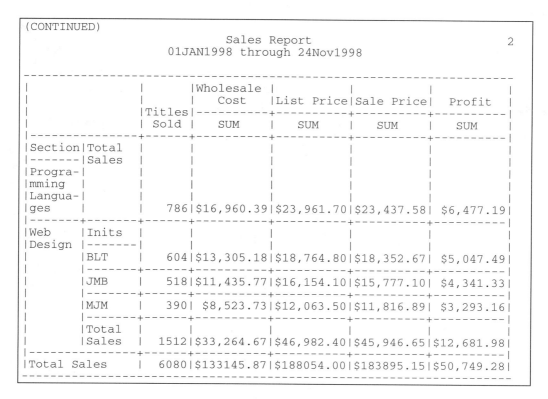

```
(CONTINUED)
                              Sales Report                        2
                      01JAN1998 through 24Nov1998

-----------------------------------------------------------------------
|               |       |Wholesale |          |          |          |
|               |       |    Cost  |List Price|Sale Price|  Profit  |
|               |Titles |----------+----------+----------+----------|
|               | Sold  |   SUM    |   SUM    |   SUM    |   SUM    |
|---------------+-------+----------+----------+----------+----------|
|Section|Total  |       |          |          |          |          |
|-------|Sales  |       |          |          |          |          |
|Progra-|       |       |          |          |          |          |
|mming  |       |       |          |          |          |          |
|Langua-|       |       |          |          |          |          |
|ges    |       |   786|$16,960.39|$23,961.70|$23,437.58| $6,477.19|
|-------+-------+-------+----------+----------+----------+----------|
|Web    |Inits  |       |          |          |          |          |
|Design |-------|       |          |          |          |          |
|       |BLT    |   604|$13,305.18|$18,764.80|$18,352.67| $5,047.49|
|       |-------+-------+----------+----------+----------+----------|
|       |JMB    |   518|$11,435.77|$16,154.10|$15,777.10| $4,341.33|
|       |-------+-------+----------+----------+----------+----------|
|       |MJM    |   390| $8,523.73|$12,063.50|$11,816.89| $3,293.16|
|       |-------+-------+----------+----------+----------+----------|
|       |Total  |       |          |          |          |          |
|       |Sales  |  1512|$33,264.67|$46,982.40|$45,946.65|$12,681.98|
|---------------+-------+----------+----------+----------+----------|
|Total Sales    |  6080|$133145.87|$188054.00|$183895.15|$50,749.28|
-----------------------------------------------------------------------
```

Enhancing the Macro Program REPORT

Numerous enhancements can be added to a macro program after completing Step 4. However, a balance needs to be made between generalizing a macro program and hard-coding features of a macro program. Each programming situation is different. For example, a macro program that will be used repeatedly for years may be worth the investment of time that it takes to enhance the macro program. A macro program that may only be used once or twice and was developed mainly as a timesaver in writing SAS code may not be worth enhancing.

Enhancements to consider adding to the macro program REPORT include the following:

- Make the data set name a parameter so that the program can be applied to other data sets.

- Check that the data set exists and that it contains observations.

- Do more error checking on the parameter values passed to the program. For instance, you may want to check that the start date is after the stop date.

- Refine the layout of the PROC TABULATE report when there are more than two classification variables.

- Improve the readability of the titles and add information to the titles: include number of observations, print the date the report was run in a different format, print the name of the data set in the title.

- Add printing options like pagesize and linesize.

- Delete the temporary data set created by the macro program.

APPENDIX A

Abridged Macro Language Reference

Appendix A summarizes macro language elements. For complete information and usage of these elements, refer to *SAS Macro Language: Reference*.

Selected SAS Options Used with the Macro Facility

Following are a number of SAS System options that can be used in conjunction with the macro facility. Most are of the on-off type. The remainder require you to specify information like librefs and filerefs. These specifications are shown in italics.

CMDMAC | NOCMDMAC

> Command-style macro programs can be invoked with command-style calls (CMDMAC).

> Command-style macro programs must be invoked with name-style calls (NOCMDMAC).

IMPLMAC | NOIMPLMAC

> Statement-style macro programs can be invoked with statement-style macro program calls (IMPLMAC).

> Statement-style macro programs must be invoked with name-style macro program calls (NOIMPLMAC).

MACRO | NOMACRO

> SAS macro facility can be used in SAS session (MACRO).

> SAS macro facility cannot be used in SAS session (NOMACRO).

MAUTOSOURCE | NOMAUTOSOURCE

> Autocall libraries will be searched when resolving macro program references (MAUTOSOURCE).

> Autocall libraries will not be searched when resolving macro program references (NOMAUTOSOURCE).

MERROR | NOMERROR

Issue warning messages when macro program references cannot be resolved (MERROR).

Do not issue warning messages when macro program references cannot be resolved (NOMERROR).

MLOGIC | NOMLOGIC

Trace execution of macro programs and write information in the SAS log (MLOGIC).

Do not trace execution of macro programs (NOMLOGIC).

MPRINT | NOMPRINT

List SAS language statements generated by macro program execution (MPRINT).

Do not list SAS language statements generated by macro program execution (NOMPRINT).

MSTORED | NOMSTORED

Search for stored compiled macros in a catalog when resolving a macro program reference. (MSTORED must be used in conjunction with SASMSTORE.) (MSTORED).

Do not search for stored compiled macros (NOMSTORED).

SASAUTOS=*library* | *(library-1, library2, ..., library-n)*

Specify one or more autocall libraries using either filerefs defined by the FILENAME statement or by enclosing each of the file names of the libraries in quotation marks.

SASMSTORE=*libref*

Specify the libref of the library that contains the catalog of stored compiled macro programs. The libref is assigned with the LIBNAME statement.

SERROR | NOSERROR

Issue warning messages when macro variable references cannot be resolved (SERROR).

Do not issue warning messages when macro variable references cannot be resolved (NOSERROR).

SYMBOLGEN | NOSYMBOLGEN

Display results of resolving macro variable references in the SAS log (SYMBOLGEN).

Do not display results of resolving macro variable references in the SAS log (NOSYMBOLGEN).

Automatic Macro Variables

All automatic macro variables except for SYSPBUFF are global macro variables. All are initialized when your SAS session starts. Host specific automatic macro variables are described in SAS documentation for the host operating system.

SQLOBS

> (type: SQL automatic macro variable)
> Set to the number of rows produced with a SELECT statement.

SQLOOPS

> (type: SQL automatic macro variable)
> Set to the number of iterations of the inner loop of PROC SQL.

SQLRC

> (type: SQL automatic macro variable)
> Set to the return code from an SQL statement.

SQLXMSG

> (type: SQL automatic macro variable)
> Set to the return code generated by a Pass-Through facility statement.

SQLXRC

> (type: SQL automatic macro variable)
> Set to the return code generated by a Pass-Through facility statement.

SYSBUFFR

> (type: read/write)
> Holds unmatched text when using the %INPUT macro language statement.

SYSCC

> (type: read only)
> Current condition code that the SAS System returns to your operating environment.

SYSCMD

> (type: read/write)
> Holds last unrecognized command from the command line of a macro window that is created with the %WINDOW macro language statement.

SYSDATE

(type: read only)
The character value that is equal to the date the SAS session started in DATE7. Format.

SYSDATE9

(type: read only [Version 7])
The character value that is equal to the date the SAS session started in DATE9. Format.

SYSDAY

(type: read only)
Text of the day of the week.

SYSDEVIC

(type: read/write)
Name of the current graphics device.

SYSDMG

(type: read only [Version 7])
Return code that reflects an action taken on a damaged data set.

SYSDSN

(type: read/write)
Name of the most recently created data set in two fields.

SYSENV

(type: read only)
The environment of the job: FORE for interactive processing and BACK for noninteractive or batch processing.

SYSERR

(type: read only by user / SAS System can modify during SAS session).
Return code set at end of each DATA step or PROC step.

SYSFILRC

(type: read only by user / SAS System can modify during SAS session)
Return code set after execution of a FILENAME statement.

SYSINDEX

(type: read only by user / SAS System can modify during SAS session)
Number of macro programs that have begun execution during the SAS session.

SYSINFO

(type: read only)
Return code information that is supplied by specific SAS procedures.

SYSJOBID

(type: read only)
Name assigned to current SAS session or batch job.

SYSLAST

(type: read/write)
Name of the most recently created data set in one field.

SYSLCKRC

(type: read only by user / SAS System can modify during SAS session)
Return code from most recent LOCK statement; used with SAS/SHARE.

SYSLIBRC

(type: read only by user / SAS System can modify during SAS session)
Return code from most recent LIBNAME statement.

SYSMENV

(type: read only by user / SAS System can modify during SAS session)
Location where the currently executing macro program was invoked: S for part of a SAS program; D for invoked from command line of a SAS window.

SYSMSG

(type: read/write)
Used in display messages in the message area in a macro window created with the %WINDOW and %DISPLAY macro language statements.

SYSPARM

(type: read/write)
Text value passed from operating system to SAS System with the SYSPARM= system option.

SYSPROCESSID

(type: read only [Version 7])
Process ID of the current SAS process.

SYSPROCESSNAME

(type: read only [Version 7])
Process name of the current SAS process.

SYSSCP

(type: read only)
Abbreviation for the operating system being used.

SYSSCPL

(type: read only)
Abbreviation for the operating system being used, usually longer than SYSSCP.

SYSSITE

(type: read only)
The character value representing your SAS site number.

SYSSTARTID

(type: read only [Version 7])
Identification number that was generated by the last STARTSAS statement.

SYSSTARTNAME

(type: read only)
Process name that was generated by the last STARTSAS statement.

SYSTIME

(type: read only)
The character value representing the time the SAS session started.

SYSUSERID

(type: read only)
User ID or login of the current SAS process.

SYSVER

(type: read only)
The character value representing the release number of SAS software that is executing.

SYSVLONG

(type: read only)
Release number and maintenance level of SAS software that is executing.

Macro Functions

Macro functions process arguments and return text values. Macro functions can be used in open code and inside macro programs. There are four types of macro functions:

- *character* functions, which operate on strings of characters or on macro variables.

- *evaluation* functions, which evaluate arithmetic and logical expressions. They temporarily convert their arguments to numbers to perform calculations and then change the results back to text.

- *quoting* functions, which mask special characters and mnemonic operators from interpretation by the macro processor.

- *other* functions, which communicate between the macro facility and the rest of the SAS System or the operating system.

In the list that follows, items you specify are in italics. Optional arguments are enclosed in brackets: (< >). Mutually exclusive items are separated with a vertical bar (|).

%BQUOTE(*argument*)

> (type: quoting)
> Masks from interpretation during execution all special characters and mnemonic operators, except for ampersands(&) and percent signs(%), in the resolved value of *argument*.
> See %NRBQUOTE.

%EVAL(*expression*)

> (type: evaluation)
> Evaluates arithmetic and logical *expressions* using integer arithmetic.

%INDEX(*source,string*)

> (type: character)
> Returns the position in *source* of the first character of *string*.

%LENGTH(*string|text expression*)

> (type: character)
> Returns the length of *string* or the length of the results of the resolution of the *text expression*.

%NRBQUOTE(*argument*)

(type: quoting)
Masks from interpretation during execution all special characters and mnemonic operators, including ampersands (&) and percent signs (%), in the resolved value of *argument*.
See %BQUOTE.

%NRSTR(*argument*)

(type: quoting)
Masks from interpretation by the macro processor during macro compilation all special characters and mnemonic operators, including ampersands (&) and percent signs (%), in *argument*.
See %STR.

%QSCAN(*argument, n <,delimiters>*)

(type: character)
Returns the nth word in *argument* where the words in *argument* are separated by *delimiters*. Masks special characters and mnemonic operators in *argument*.
See %SCAN.

%QSUBSTR(*argument, position <,length>*)

(type: character)
Extracts a substring of *length* characters from *argument* starting at *position* and masks special characters and mnemonic operators in *argument*.
See %SUBSTR.

%QSYSFUNC(*function(argument(s)) <,format>*)

(type: other)
Executes SAS language *function* or user-written *function* and returns the results to the macro facility (see also macro statement %SYSCALL). Masks special characters and mnemonic operators from interpretation by the macro processor.
See %SYSFUNC.

%QUPCASE(*string|text expression*)

(type: quoting)
Converts *string* or *text expression* to upper case and masks special characters and mnemonic operators in *string* or *text expression* from interpretation by the macro processor.
See %UPCASE.

%SCAN(*argument, n <,delimiters>*)

(type: character)
Returns the nth word in *argument* where the words in *argument* are separated by *delimiters*.
See %QSCAN.

%STR(*argument*)

(type: quoting)
Masks from interpretation by the macro processor during macro compilation all special characters and mnemonic operators, except for ampersands(&) and percent signs(%), in *argument*.
See %NRSTR.

%SUBSTR(*argument, position <,length>*)

(type: character)
Extracts a substring of *length* characters from *argument* starting at *position*.
See %QSUBSTR.

%SUPERQ(*macro-variable*)

(type: quoting)
Masks from interpretation by the macro processor at execution all special characters and mnemonic operators, including ampersands(&) and percent signs (%), in the value of *macro-variable*.

%SYSEVALF(*expression <,conversion-type>*)

(type: evaluation)
Where *conversion-type* is BOOLEAN, CEIL, FLOOR, or INTEGER.
Evaluate arithmetic and logical *expressions* using floating-point arithmetic. Optionally converts results to *conversion-type*.

%SYSFUNC(*function(argument(s)) <,format>*)

(type: other)
Executes SAS language *function* or user-written *function* and returns the results to the macro facility (see also macro statement %SYSCALL).
See %QSYSFUNC.

%SYSGET(*host-environment-variable*)

(type: other)
Returns the value of *host-environment-variable* to the macro facility.

%SYSPROD(*SAS-product*)

(type: other)
Returns a code to indicate whether *SAS-product* is licensed at the site where the SAS System is currently running.

%UNQUOTE(*argument*)

(type: quoting)
Unmasks all special characters and mnemonic operators in *argument* during macro execution.

%UPCASE(*string|text expression*)

(type: quoting)
Converts *string* or *text expression* to upper case.
See %QUPCASE.

Macro Language Statements

The statements in the macro language are listed below. The information that you specify is indicated in italics. Optional information is enclosed in brackets < >.

There are two types of macro language statements:

- statements that can be executed in open code and within a macro program

- statements that can be executed only from inside a macro program.

In the following list, items that you specify are in italics. Optional arguments are enclosed in brackets < >.

%* *comment*;

> (type: open code/inside)
> Where comment is a string of any length.
> Adds descriptive text to your macro programming.

%DISPLAY *window* <*.group*> <*NOINPUT*> <*BLANK*> <*BELL*> <*DELETE*>;

> (type: open code/ inside)
> Displays a macro window defined with %WINDOW that can display fields and accept user input.

%DO;

> (type: inside)
> Signals the beginning of a %DO group; the statements that follow form a block of code that is terminated with a %END statement.

%DO, iterative

> (type: inside)
> Repetitively executes a section of macro code by using an index variable and the keywords %TO and %BY; the section of macro code is terminated with a %END statement.
> %DO *macro-variable=start* %TO *stop* <%BY *increment*>;
>
> > *text and macro program statements*
>
> %END;

where:

> *start* and *stop* are integers or macro expressions that define the bounds of the iterative %DO
>
> *increment* is an integer or macro expression that defines the increment to take from *start* to reach *stop*.

%DO %UNTIL (*expression*);

(type: inside)
Repetitively executes a section of macro code *until* the macro *expression* that follows the %UNTIL is true; the section of macro code is terminated with a %END statement. Because the expression is evaluated at the bottom of the loop, a %DO %UNTIL loop always executes at least once.
%DO %UNTIL (*expression*);

> *text and macro program statements*

%END;

%DO %WHILE (*expression*);

(type: inside)
Repetitively executes a section of macro code *while* the macro expression that follows the %WHILE is true; the section of macro code is terminated with a %END statement. Because the expression is evaluated at the top of the loop, a %DO %WHILE may not execute.
%DO %WHILE (*expression*);

> *text and macro program statements*

%END;

%END;

(type: inside)
Terminates a %DO group.

%GLOBAL *macro-variable-1 macro-variable-2 ... macro-variable-n*;

(type: open code/inside)
Creates and identifies macro variables that are to be available throughout the SAS session and stored in the global symbol table.

%GOTO *label*;

(type: inside)
Branches macro processing to the specified macro *label* within the macro program.

%IF-%THEN/%ELSE

(type: inside)

Conditionally processes a section of a macro program that follows %THEN when the result of the macro expression that follows %IF is true; when the macro expression that follows %IF is false and %ELSE is specified, the section of macro code following the %ELSE is executed. Multiple %ELSE statements for different conditions can be specified.

%IF *expression* %THEN *macro-expression*;

<%ELSE *macro-expression*;>

%INPUT *<macro-variable-1 macro-variable-2 ... macro-variable-n>*;

(type: open code/inside)

Accepts input as entered by the user or by the program and updates macro variables with the values entered.

%label: *macro-text*

(type: inside)

Identifies a section of macro code; typically used as the destination of a %GOTO statement.

%KEYDEF *key-name <definition>*;

(type: open code/inside)

Assigns a definition to a function key.

%LET *macro-variable=<value>*;

(type: open code/inside)

Creates a macro variable and/or assign it a value.

%LOCAL *macro-variable-1 macro-variable-2 ... macro-variable-n*;

(type: inside)

Defines macro variables that are available only to the macro program in which the %LOCAL statement was issued.

%MACRO *name <(parameter-list)> < / <CMD> <DES='text'> <PARMBUFF> <STMT> <STORE> >*;

> (type: open code/inside)
> Begins the definition of a macro program.
> where:
>
>> *name* is the name of the macro program.
>>
>> *parameter-list* can contain either positional parameters or keyword parameters or both. If both, the positional parameters must come first.
>>
>> *CMD* specifies that the macro program can be invoked with either a name-style or command-style invocation.
>>
>> *DES='text'* adds descriptive *text* to the macro program when stored in a macro catalog.
>>
>> *PARMBUFF* (or *PBUFF*) assigns the entire list of parameter values in the call to the macro program to an automatic macro variable named SYSPBUFF.
>>
>> *STMT* specifies that the macro program can be invoked with either a name-style invocation or a statement-style invocation.
>>
>> *STORE* specifies that the compiled macro program should be stored in a SAS catalog.

%MEND;

> (type: inside)
> Terminates a macro program definition.

%PUT *<text> <_ALL_> <_AUTOMATIC_> <_GLOBAL_> <_LOCAL_> <_USER_>*;

> (type: open code/ inside)
> Writes text or macro variable values to the SAS log,
> where:
>
>> *text* is text or a macro variable reference.
>>
>> *_ALL_* lists the values of all automatic and user-defined macro variables.
>>
>> *_AUTOMATIC_* lists the values of all automatic macro variables.
>>
>> *_GLOBAL_* lists the values of user-defined global macro variables.
>>
>> *_LOCAL_* lists the values of user-defined macro variables within the currently executing macro program.
>>
>> *_USER_* lists the user-defined global and local macro variables.

%SYSCALL *call-routine <(call-routine-arguments)>*;

> (type: open code/inside)
> Invokes a SAS System or user-defined CALL routine.

%SYSEXEC *<command>*;

> (type: open code/inside)
> Issues a *command* to the operating system. If you omit *command*, you are placed in operating system mode. %SYSEXEC is operating system dependent.

%SYSRPUT *local-macro-variable=remote-macro-variable*;

> (type: open code/ inside)
> Assigns the value of a macro variable on the remote host to a local macro variable.

%WINDOW *window-name <window-options>group-definition-1 <...group-definition-n>*;

> (type: open code/ inside)
> Defines a customized window to display text and accept user input.

PROC SQL Interface to the Macro Facility

The INTO clause on the SELECT statement creates and updates macro variables. The information on the INTO clause that you specify is indicated in italics. Optional information is enclosed in brackets < >.

SELECT col1,col2,...

      INTO *:macro-variable-specification-1*

        <,:macro-variable-specification-2,..., macro-variable-n>

      FROM table-expression

      WHERE where-expression

      other clauses;

create or update macro variables with values that are produced by PROC SQL,

where:

- macro variables can be listed

    :macro-variable-1, :macro-variable2, ..., :macro-variable-n

- macro variables can be written in a numeric list

    :macro-variable-1-:macro-variable-n

- values that are placed in a macro variable can be side-by-side and separated with a character when SEPARATED BY clause is added:

    SEPARATED BY *'character'*

The NOTRIM option can be added to prevent leading and trailing blanks from being removed when the macro variable is created.

    :macro-variable-1 notrim

SAS Functions and Routines that Interface with the Macro Facility

The four functions and routines in the SAS language and the SCL functions that interface with the macro facility are described in this section. The information that you specify is indicated in italics.

SYMGET(*argument*)

retrieves a *macro-variable* value for use in a DATA step,

where *argument* can be one of the following:

- literal text that is enclosed in quotation marks
- the name of a data set character variable whose values are the names of macro variables
- a character expresssion that resolves to a macro variable name.

SYMGETN(*'macro-variable'*)

SCL function that retrieves a *macro-variable* value and stores it as a number,

where the *macro-variable* name can be specified one of two ways:

- the actual *macro-variable* name enclosed in single quotes with no leading ampersand (&)
- the name of an SCL variable that contains the name of the *macro-variable.*

CALL SYMPUT(*macro-variable,value*)

creates or updates a macro variable from within a DATA step,

where the *macro-variable* name can be specified one of the following ways:

- literal text that is enclosed in quotation marks
- the name of a DATA step character variable whose values are the names of macro variables
- a character expresssion that resolves to a macro variable name.

where *value* can be specified one of the following ways:

- literal text enclosed in quotation marks
- the name of a DATA step variable (character or numeric)
- a DATA step expression.

CALL SYMPUTN(*'macro-variable'*,*value*)

SCL routine that assigns a numeric value to a macro variable,

where the *macro-variable* name can be specified one of two ways:

- the actual *macro-variable* name enclosed in single quotes with no leading ampersand (&)
- the name of an SCL variable that contains the name of the *macro-variable*.

CALL EXECUTE(*argument*)

executes the resolved value of *argument* from within a DATA step. Resolved values are usually macro facility references,

where *argument* can be one of the following:

- a character string enclosed in single or double quotation marks. Single quotation marks direct resolution to occur during execution of the DATA step. Double quotation marks direct resolution to occur before the DATA step is compiled.
- the name of a DATA step variable.
- a character expression that is resolved by the DATA step to a text expression.

RESOLVE(*argument*)

resolves *argument* during DATA step execution. The *argument* is a text expression that is resolved by the macro facility,

where *argument* can be one of the following:

- a character string enclosed in single quotation marks
- the name of a DATA step variable
- a character expression that is resolved by the DATA step to a text expression.

APPENDIX B

Reserved Words in the Macro Facility

The following words are reserved for use by the macro facility.

Do not use a reserved word to name a macro program, a macro variable, or a macro label. When a reserved word is used in the macro facility, the macro processor issues a warning and the macro program is not processed.

Do not start the name of a macro program, macro variable, or macro label with SYS, AF, or DMS. The SYS prefix is used by the SAS System to name many of the automatic variables.

ABEND	COMANDR	EDIT	INC
ABORT	COPY	ELSE	INCLUDE
ACT	DEACT	END	INDEX
ACTIVATE	DEL	EVAL	INFILE
BQUOTE	DELETE	FILE	INPUT
BY	DISPLAY	GLOBAL	KEYDEF
CLEAR	DMIDSPLY	GO	LENGTH
CLOSE	DMISPLIT	GOTO	LET
CMS	DO	IF	LIST
LISTM	PUT	STOP	TO
LOCAL	QSCAN	STR	TSO
MACRO	QSUBST	SUBSTR	UNQUOTE
MEND	QUOTE	SUPERQ	UNSTR
METASYM	QSYSFUNC	SYSCALL	UNTIL
NRBQUOTE	QUPCASE	SYSEVALF	UPCASE
NRQUOTE	RESOLVE	SYSEXEC	WHILE
NRSTR	RETURN	SYSFUNC	WINDOW
ON	RUN	SYSGET	
OPEN	SAVE	SYSRPUT	
PAUSE	SCAN	THEN	

APPENDIX C

Sample Data Set

The following DATA step creates the data set that is used in this book.

```
data books.ytdsales;

   keep section--salepric;
   attrib section   length=$26 label='Section'
          saleid    length=8 label='Sale ID'
                    format=8.
          saleinit  length=$3 label='Sales Person Initials'
          datesold  length=4 label='Date Book Sold'
                    format=mmddyy8. informat=mmddyy8.
          title     length=$50 label='Title of Book'
          author    length=$50 label='First Author'
          publishr  length=$50 label='Publisher'
          cost      length=8 label='Wholesale Cost'
                    format=dollar9.2
          listpric  length=8 label='List Price'
                    format=dollar9.2
          salepric  length=8 label='Sale Price'
                    format=dollar9.2;

   array jan{5} jan1-jan5 (105,40,110,60,85);
   array feb{5} feb1-feb5 (120,40,130,45,150);
   array mar{5} mar1-mar5 (115,60,175,75,145);
   array apr{5} apr1-apr5 (145,55,132,60,131);
   array may{5} may1-may5 (190,60,165,90,135);
   array jun{5} jun1-jun5 (160,56,168,84,143);
   array jul{5} jul1-jul5 (138,50,149,72,140);
   array aug{5} aug1-aug5 (139,40,153,68,142);
   array sep{5} sep1-sep5 (150,58,159,80,150);
   array oct{5} oct1-oct5 (157,52,163,83,155);
   array nov{5} nov1-nov5 (168,63,173,88,170);
   array dec{5} dec1-dec5 (190,75,200,95,210);

   array mos{60} jan1--dec5;

   array momax{12} momax1-momax12
                 (30,27,30,29,30,29,30,30,29,30,29,30);

   array sname{5} $ 26 ('Internet' 'Networks and Communication'
                  'Operating Systems'
                  'Programming Languages' 'Web Design');
```

```
   array prices{13} p1-p13
                    (15,18,19,22,24,28,29,32,35,39,42,41,76);

   do m=1 to 12;
     do i=1 to 5;
       section=sname{i};
       do j=1 to mos{(m-1)*5+i};
         day=round(momax{m}*uniform(3),1)+1;
         datesold=mdy(m,day,1998);
         title=trim(sname{i}) || ' Title ' || put(j,3.);
         pval=round(2*normal(3),1) + 7;
         if pval > 13 then pval=13;
         else if pval < 1 then pval=1;
         listpric=prices{pval} + .95;
         salepric=listpric;
         if mod(j,8)=0 then salepric=listpric*.9;
         if mod(j,17)=0 and mod(j,8) ne 0
           then salepric=listpric*.8;
         cost=.7*listpric;
         if mod(j,12)=0 then cost=.8*listpric;
         person=mod(day,3);
         if mod(day,12)=0 then person=1;
         if mod(day,20)=0 then person=2;
         if mod(day,15)=0 then person=0;
         if person=0 then saleinit='MJM';
         else if person=1 then saleinit='BLT';
         else if person=2 then saleinit='JMB';
         output;
       end;
     end;
   end;
run;
```

The PROC CONTENTS of the sample data set follows.

```
Data Set Name:   BOOKS.YTDSALES        Observations:          6959
Member Type:     DATA                  Variables:               10
Engine:          V612                  Indexes:                  0
Created:         11:21 Fri, Jul 10, 98 Observation Length:     215
Last Modified:   11:21 Fri, Jul 10, 98 Deleted Observations:     0
Protection:                            Compressed:              NO
Data Set Type:                         Sorted:                  NO
Label:

           -----Engine/Host Dependent Information-----

              Data Set Page Size:        8192
              Number of Data Set Pages:  184
              File Format:               607
              First Data Page:           1
              Max Obs per Page:          38
              Obs in First Data Page:    30

        -----Alphabetic List of Variables and Attributes-----

 # Variable  Type Len Pos Format      Informat  Label
 ---------------------------------------------------------------
  6 AUTHOR   Char  50  91                        First Author
  8 COST     Num    8 191 DOLLAR9.2              Wholesale Cost
  4 DATESOLD Num    4  37 MMDDYY8.    MMDDYY8.   Date Book Sold
  9 LISTPRIC Num    8 199 DOLLAR9.2              List Price
  7 PUBLISHR Char  50 141                        Publisher
  2 SALEID   Num    8  26 8.                     Sale ID
  3 SALEINIT Char   3  34                        Sales Person
Initials
 10 SALEPRIC Num    8 207 DOLLAR9.2              Sale Price
  1 SECTION  Char  26   0                        Section
  5 TITLE    Char  50  41                        Title of Book
```

Glossary

This section contains a glossary of macro language terms.

autocall facility

> a feature of the SAS System that enables you to store the source statements that define a macro program and invoke the macro program as needed without explicitly including the macro program code in your program.

automatic macro variable

> a macro variable defined by the SAS System when your SAS session starts.

calling a macro program

> see macro invocation

compilation

> the process of checking syntax for errors and translating program code into a form that the computer can execute.

execution

> the process of performing the actions defined in a portion of a program (such as a DATA step or PROC step or a macro program)

global macro symbol table

> the area where the macro processor stores global macro variables.

global macro variable

> a macro variable that can be referenced anywhere in a SAS program, including in open code and within a macro program. The reference may be blocked in a macro program if a local macro variable exists with the same name. A global macro variable exists until the end of the program.

input stack

> the area where a program goes after being submitted and while it waits processing by the word scanner

invoking a macro

> see macro invocation

keyword parameter

> a macro program parameter defined with an equal sign after the parameter name as in *parameter-name=*.

local macro symbol table

> the area where the macro processor stores macro variables created within a macro program that have not been defined as global.

local macro variable

> a macro variable created within a macro program that is available only within the macro program and macro programs called from within the macro program. A local macro variable ceases to exist when the macro program that created it ends.

macro program, or macro

> the macro language statements taken together that make up a unit. A macro program can be compiled and executed to do many programming tasks including: generating SAS statements, display manager commands, and macro language statements; writing messages to the SAS log; accepting input; creating or changing the values of macro variables.

macro call

> see macro invocation

macro compilation

> the process of converting a macro program definition from the statements you enter into a form that the macro processor can use for execution.

macro execution

> the process of following the instructions given by compiled macro program statements.

macro facility

> a portion of the SAS System used for extending and customizing the SAS System. It consists of the macro processor and macro language.

macro invocation

> an instruction to the macro processor to execute a macro program. It is also known as a macro call.

macro language

> the programming language you use to communicate with the macro processor.

macro parameter

> a local macro variable defined in parentheses on the %MACRO statement. Macro parameters initialize macro variables when a macro program is called.

macro processor

the portion of the SAS System that compiles and executes macro program statements and macro programs.

macro quoting

see the entry for quoting.

macro variable

a variable belonging to the macro language whose value is text that remains constant until you change it.

macro variable reference

the name of a macro variable preceded by an ampersand (&) that the macro processor replaces with the value assigned to the macro variable.

masking

see the entry for quoting.

mnemonic operator

an arithmetic or logical operator composed of letters rather than symbols (e.g. EQ rather than =).

null value

a value consisting of 0 characters.

open code

the part of a SAS program outside any macro program definition.

parameter

see the entry for macro parameter

positional parameter

a parameter that is defined by name only and whose value is assigned by matching the parameter in a particular position in the %MACRO statement with the value in the corresponding position in the call to the macro program.

quoting

the process that causes the macro processor to treat certain items as text rather than as symbols for interpretation in the macro language. Quoting masks the item from view by the macro processor.

quoting function

a macro language function that performs quoting on its argument.

resolving a macro variable reference

the process of replacing a macro variable reference with the value of that macro variable.

SAS compilation

the process of converting SAS language statements from the form in which you enter them into a form that the SAS System can use for execution.

SAS execution

the process of following the instructions given by compiled SAS language statements to perform an action.

step boundary

a point in a SAS program where the SAS System recognizes that a DATA step or PROC step is complete.

string

any group of characters.

symbol table

the area in which the macro processor stores macro variables.

token

the unit in the SAS System into which SAS language statements and macro language statements must be broken in order to be processed.

tokenizer

the part of the word scanner that breaks input into tokens.

unquoting

the process of restoring the meaning of an item previously quoted.

word scanner

a part of the SAS System that examines all tokens in a SAS program and directs the destination of the tokens. For example, the word scanner can send tokens to the DATA step compiler or the macro processor.

References

SAS Institute, Inc., (1990), *SAS Guide to Macro Processing, Version 6, Second Edition,* Cary, NC: SAS Institute, Inc.

SAS Institute, Inc., (1994), *SAS Macro Facility Tips and Techniques, Version 6, First Edition,* Cary, NC: SAS Institute, Inc.

SAS Institute, Inc., (1996), *SAS Macro Language Course Notes,* Cary, NC: SAS Institute, Inc.

SAS Institute, Inc., (1997), *SAS Macro Language: Reference, First Edition,* Cary, NC: SAS Institute, Inc.

Other sources of SAS macro programming information:

The *SAS Users Group International Conference Proceedings,* published annually, usually contains several papers dealing with macro programming issues.

The online journal *Observations: The Technical Journal for SAS Software Users* occasionally has articles related to the macro facility. This journal is available through the SAS Institute web page: www.sas.com. The hardcopy version of *Observations* published until 1997 carried several articles about macro programming.

Index

Call your local SAS® office to order these other books and tapes available through the Books by Users℠ program:

An Array of Challenges — Test Your SAS® Skills
by **Robert Virgile**..................................Order No. A55625

Applied Multivariate Statistics with SAS® Software
by **Ravindra Khattree**
and **Dayanand N. Naik**........................Order No. A55234

Applied Statistics and the SAS® Programming Language, Fourth Edition
by **Ronald P. Cody**
and **Jeffrey K. Smith**...........................Order No. A55984

Beyond the Obvious with SAS® Screen Control Language
by **Don Stanley** ....Order No. A55073

Carpenter's Complete Guide to the SAS® Macro Language
by **Art Carpenter** ....Order No. A56100

The Cartoon Guide to Statistics
by **Larry Gonick**
and **Woollcott Smith**...........................Order No. A55153

Categorical Data Analysis Using the SAS® System
by **Maura E. Stokes, Charles S. Davis,**
and **Gary G. Koch** ....Order No. A55320

Common Statistical Methods for Clinical Research with SAS® Examples
by **Glenn A. Walker**..............................Order No. A55991

Concepts and Case Studies in Data Management
by **William S. Calvert**
and **J. Meimei Ma**................................Order No. A55220

Efficiency: Improving the Performance of Your SAS® Applications
by **Robert Virgile**..................................Order No. A55960

Essential Client/Server Survival Guide, Second Edition
by **Robert Orfali, Dan Harkey,**
and **Jeri Edwards**.................................Order No. A56285

Extending SAS® Survival Analysis Techniques for Medical Research
by **Alan Cantor**....................................Order No. A55504

A Handbook of Statistical Analyses using SAS®
by **B.S. Everitt**
and **G. Der** ....Order No. A56378

The How-To Book for SAS/GRAPH® Software
by **Thomas Miron** ....Order No. A55203

In the Know ... SAS® Tips and Techniques From Around the Globe
by **Phil Mason** ....Order No. A55513

Integrating Results through Meta-Analytic Review Using SAS® Software
by **Morgan C. Wang** and
Brad J. Bushman ....Order No. A55810

Learning SAS® in the Computer Lab
by **Rebecca J. Elliott** ....Order No. A55273

The Little SAS® Book: A Primer
by **Lora D. Delwiche** and
Susan J. Slaughter ....Order No. A55200

The Little SAS® Book: A Primer, Second Edition
by **Lora D. Delwiche** and
Susan J. Slaughter ....Order No. A56649
(updated to include Version 7 features)

Mastering the SAS® System, Second Edition
by **Jay A. Jaffe** ....Order No. A55123

The Next Step: Integrating the Software Life Cycle with SAS® Programming
by **Paul Gill** ....Order No. A55697

Painless Windows 3.1: A Beginner's Handbook for SAS® Users
by **Jodie Gilmore** ....Order No. A55505

Painless Windows: A Handbook for SAS® Users
by **Jodie Gilmore** ....Order No. A55769

Professional SAS® Programmers Pocket Reference, Second Edition
by **Rick Aster** ....Order No. A56646

*Welcome * Bienvenue * Willkommen * Yohkoso * Bienvenido*

SAS® Publications Is Easy to Reach

Visit our SAS Publications Web page located at www.sas.com/pubs

You will find product and service details, including

- **sample chapters**
- **tables of contents**
- **author biographies**
- **book reviews**

Learn about

- **regional user groups conferences**
- **trade show sites and dates**
- **authoring opportunities**
- **custom textbooks**

Order books with ease at our secured Web page!

Explore all the services that Publications has to offer!

Your Listserv Subscription Brings the News to You Automatically

Do you want to be among the first to learn about the latest books and services available from SAS Publications? Subscribe to our listserv **newdocnews-l** and automatically receive the following once each month: a description of the new titles, the applicable environments or operating systems, and the applicable SAS release(s). To subscribe:

1. Send an e-mail message to **listserv@vm.sas.com**

2. Leave the "Subject" line blank

3. Use the following text for your message:

    subscribe newdocnews-l *your-first-name your-last-name*

    For example: subscribe newdocnews-l John Doe

    Please note: newdocnews-l ⟵_____ that's the letter "l" not the number "1".

For customers outside the U.S., contact your local SAS office for listserv information.

Create Customized Textbooks Quickly, Easily, and Affordably

SelecText® offers instructors at U.S. colleges and universities a way to create custom textbooks for courses that teach students how to use SAS software.

For more information, see our Web page at **www.sas.com/selectext**, or contact our SelecText coordinators by sending e-mail to **selectext@sas.com**.

You're Invited to Publish with SAS Institute's User Publishing Program

If you enjoy writing about SAS software and how to use it, the User Publishing Program at SAS Institute Inc. offers a variety of publishing options. We are actively recruiting authors to publish books, articles, and sample code. Do you find the idea of writing a book or an article by yourself a little intimidating? Consider writing with a co-author. Keep in mind that you will receive complete editorial and publishing support, access to our users, technical advice and assistance, and competitive royalties. Please contact us for an author packet. E-mail us at **sasbbu@sas.com** or call 919-677-8000, then press 1-6479. See the SAS Publications Web page at **www.sas.com/pubs** for complete information.

Read All about It in *Authorline*®!

Our User Publishing newsletter, *Authorline*, features author interviews, conference news, and informational updates and highlights from our User Publishing Program. Published quarterly, *Authorline* is available free of charge. To subscribe, send e-mail to **sasbbu@sas.com** or call 919-677-8000, then press 1-6479.

See *Observations*®, Our Online Technical Journal

Feature articles from *Observations*®: *The Technical Journal for SAS*® *Software Users* are now available online at **www.sas.com/obs**. Take a look at what your fellow SAS software users and SAS Institute experts have to tell you. You may decide that you, too, have information to share. If you are interested in writing for *Observations*, send e-mail to **sasbbu@sas.com** or call 919-677-8000, then press 1-6479.

Book Discount Offered at SAS Public Training Courses!

When you attend one of our SAS Public Training Courses at any of our regional Training Centers in the U.S., you will receive a 15% discount on any book orders placed during the course. Each course has a list of recommended books to choose from, and the books are displayed for you to see. Take advantage of this offer at the next course you attend!

SAS Institute
SAS Campus Drive
Cary, NC 27513-2414
Fax 919-677-4444

E-mail: sasbook@sas.com
Web page: www.sas.com/pubs
To order books, call Fulfillment Services at 800-727-3228*
For other SAS Institute business, call 919-677-8000*

* Note: Customers outside the U.S. should contact their local SAS office.